THE DR. DE BETZ
CHAMPAGNE
DIET

THE DR. DE BETZ
CHAMPAGNE
DIET

The Medically Proven Program for Total Weight Control

Barbara DeBetz, M.D., and
Samm Sinclair Baker

CROWN PUBLISHERS, INC.
NEW YORK

Publisher's Note: This book contains diet instructions to be followed within the context of a complete weight-loss program. However, not all diets are designed for all individuals. Before starting this or any other diet or weight-loss program a physician should be consulted. The instructions in this work are not intended as a substitute for professional medical advice.

Copyright © 1987 by Barbara DeBetz, M.D., and Samm Sinclair Baker

Published by Crown Publishers, Inc., 225 Park Avenue South, New York, New York 10003 and represented in Canada by the Canadian Manda Group.

CROWN is a trademark of Crown Publishers, Inc.

Manufactured in the United States of America

Library of Congress Cataloging-in-Publication Data

DeBetz, Barbara.
  The Dr. DeBetz champagne diet.

  Includes index.
  1. Reducing diets. 2. Reducing—Psychological
aspects. I. Baker, Samm Sinclair. II. Title.
III. Title: Doctor DeBetz champagne diet.
IV. Title: champagne diet.
RM222.2.D426   1987   613.2'5   86-16804

ISBN 0-517-56416-5

10 9 8 7 6 5 4 3 2 1

First Edition

To my patients with gratitude and appreciation.

BARBARA DE BETZ, M.D.

To Natalie, my indispensable working partner in this book and in everything else worthwhile.

SAMM SINCLAIR BAKER

CONTENTS

THE DR. DE BETZ
CHAMPAGNE
DIET

1

HOW I DEVELOPED THE TWO-WAY TOUCH-CONTROL DIET SYSTEM

It Works and Keeps Working for You Lifelong

I recognized early in my medical career that something absolutely necessary was missing from every reducing program to date. In over 16 years of medical practice, I've proved that overweight women and men need not only a tested effective diet, but also an easy-to-use support method, a backup system to stop from breaking the diet, and then to block regaining lost pounds. To meet the need, I developed my total-control, two-way system, combining the advanced DeBetz Diet with my carefully researched touch-control action.

This revolutionary combination has worked wonderfully for hundreds upon hundreds of my formerly overweight patients. It will work for you if you work with it. With the built-in double benefit, this book can help you achieve better health, better looks, and maximum well-being.

Skeptical? I don't blame you. My highly successful two-way method is radically different from any other diet. It may seem confusing until you try it and see how logically and simply it works. So it's intelligent to ask, "How can the touch of a finger possibly reduce me?" It can't. But you *can* reduce, as never possible for you before, with the combination of my diet teamed with touch-control. Tested and proved, here's how it works:

1. The DeBetz Diet's eating plan *takes off* your excess weight.
2. The 20-second touch-control action and STOPlines *keep you dieting* until you're slim.

Diet alone can't do it; touch-control alone can't do it. The combination will help you reduce and keep you trim no matter how many times you may have failed before. You failed because you never had the combination two-way method before.

Why is touch-control indispensable? One answer is in the story of the screaming, out-of-control child (like the out-of-control dieter) whose frantic parents called in a famous doctor. He took one look, then slammed his hands together in a resounding *crack*—and the tantrum stopped instantly. The amazed mother asked, "But aren't you supposed to reason with him and teach him?" "Sure," the doctor explained, "but first you have to get his attention."

Similarly, the touch-control action focuses your attention and stops you instantly from grabbing fattening food and breaking your diet. That's why my diet-plus-touch system will work for you as it has for so many of my overweight patients. Try it—you have nothing to lose but your overweight.

Also, you'll love the bubbly lift of a daily optional glass of Champagne or other sparkling drink of your choice, as instructed in chapter 4. Like other delighted, newly slim dieters, you'll call this "the first *civilized* diet," the "happy diet," "the *celebration* diet," as you celebrate steady weight loss day after day. You'll find that my sparkling diet will help make you feel light and cheery, with a general sense of well-being physically and psychologically. Each day your scale will assure you silently, "*Have a happy weigh.*"

PROVED IN PRACTICE

My records prove that the many overweight women and men I've treated, of varying ages and types, succeeded in reducing and staying trim, no matter how many times they had failed on one-dimensional diet programs in the past. Follow-up reports confirm that they were able at last to keep that overweight off year after year.

Doctors began referring hard-to-reduce patients to me. Newly slim individuals told others about touch-control benefits. The word spread—and this book is the result, fulfilling my desire to help overweight individuals everywhere.

A typical example from my practice is Dorothy Nystrom, a hospital supervisor, who told me at the start, "I'm over 160 pounds, have been trying for years to get down to 125, but nothing works for me. Do you know why I'm fat? It's because I eat out of frustration, anxiety, and tension, and that spells f-a-t."

She went on, "Frankly, I'm very skeptical about this 'touch-control.' It's so far out, I never heard of anything like it. But it has worked for friends who reduced for the first time in their lives. I'm desperate. I'll try anything."

After using my two-way system, the day came when Mrs. Nystrom phoned and said:

"I was amazed and delighted that your diet–touch system started working for me immediately. The first time I used the stop signal, it stopped me from snatching a fattening jelly doughnut. And nobody noticed I was using the stop action. It has stopped me hundreds of times since from breaking my diet. I've lost weight steadily. I stepped on my scale this morning and saw that I reached my 125-pound goal, 35 pounds lighter than when we met. I'm thrilled!"

As I congratulated her, she added, "I did it! I finally changed from f-a-t to s-l-i-m." She has called me for the past four years and said, "I'm still s-l-i-m, haven't gained an ounce." You'll be able to say the same.

STARTS WORKING RIGHT AWAY

The two-way method will start working for you at once, breaking bad eating and overeating habits just as applying a brake stops a runaway car. *You'll lose up to five pounds or more a week,* depending on how overweight you are. Then you'll lose more pounds steadily until down to your desired weight. But the methods you'll learn don't stop there.

After you've trimmed down, you'll have the two-way touch-control system at your fingertips to use whenever needed to turn off temptation and keep unwanted pounds from creeping back. Instead of being driven by food, you'll do the driving. For the rest of your life, the 20 seconds of touch-control peak concentration will become as natural to you as breathing, will fortify your resistance to "fat eating" and overeating. You're sure then that you'll stay trim always. *You'll never be overweight again.*

DIET PLUS TOUCH-STOP-SUPPORT AIDS EQUALS WEIGHT-CONTROL SUCCESS

Understand that just touching your face won't automatically make unwanted fat and flab disappear. Any such claim or expectation would be unreal. The touch is a carefully developed action tool that *physically* activates the *emotional* control you need to keep from giving in to temptation and falling off the diet.

The touch-action tool puts into effect for you the stop and support procedures, which you'll learn quickly. The stop system stops you from grabbing diet-breaking food and from overloading. The support boost keeps you dieting down to your desired weight—and then from regaining lost pounds. The coordinated steps have been thoroughly, scientifically tested and proved effective. *And nobody around will know when you use the procedure.*

The simple reminder can work for you as it did for Walter T. Strauss, an advertising executive, who told me, "I'm 44, and was always proud of my trim, athletic body. Gradually I put on 25 extra pounds, became fat and flabby. None of the diets I tried worked for me. Then I followed a formerly overweight friend to your offices.

"It was hard for me to believe that your revolutionary system would work . . . until I tried it. Then it was one of my greatest thrills, that a fingertip touch could help stop me from snacking and overeating. Touch-control with your diet took off the 25 pounds of flab. I've kept trim and vigorous for two years now. Business lunches and social dinners don't scare me any longer.

"Just yesterday, for instance, during a conference with a dozen associates, at the coffee break around the long table, I resisted the sweet rolls by using the stop action. I touched my forehead as though thinking deeply—and no one noticed. My two buddies, stop and support, keep me honest. I'm sure I'll never be overweight again."

QUICK TEST:
TOUCH AND GO DOWN IN WEIGHT

I'd like you to try this quick touch action for a few seconds right now, just as I've instructed so many overweight patients eager to reduce. You'll enjoy it.

To begin, reach out with a fingertip and touch any part of your face lightly—let's say your cheek. Delight in the intimate contact, the warmth of instant connection and communication of skin against skin. That *concentration* of sensation in both body and mind is a key element of effective touch-control. The touch feels good, doesn't it? Realize that in touching your face, especially near the mouth, you're focusing on your intimate eating area. The touch is gentle and protective—in dramatic contrast to putting excessive food into your mouth, which is destructive.

You'll learn how to coordinate the physical touch with the three brief STOPlines that you'll be repeating as your totally personal signal to yourself, as often as needed from now on. Each time you touch you'll be reminding yourself that you're progressing with steady, sure weight reduction and the encouraging confidence of being in control on your diet. Then you'll reinforce your steady, continuing weight loss by touching and repeating the special SUPPORTlines.

Never forget that the bottom line of successful reducing and lasting slimness is this: Diet alone is not enough; touch-control itself is not enough. Only the proved two-way system—diet teamed with touch-control—will keep you losing pounds steadily until you're down to your desired weight. Once trim, you go on using touch-control as you wish, coupled with your lifelong blueprint guide (chapter 11), to keep looking and feeling your best year after year.

HOW I DEVELOPED THE TWO-WAY SYSTEM

While growing up, before starting my medical training, I had to fight my own overweight problem repeatedly. That added urgency to my desire to develop a new treatment that would be medically sound, effective, and lasting. Working with colleagues in medical school and hospitals, and in thorough M.D. and psychiatric training, I concentrated especially on the understanding and treatment of eating disorders, overweight in particular.

As a medical doctor, psychiatrist, and bariatrician (I'm a member of the American Society of Bariatric Physicians, which is concerned primarily with weight control), I saw patients who had tried everything. They had been involved with many diets, self-help groups, various behavior modification programs, acupuncture, jaw wiring, other treatments—and they had failed. It soon became increasingly clear to me that the primary problem was not that most of them didn't lose some weight, but they failed overall for two reasons:

1. They couldn't keep their motivation long enough to really slim down to their ideal weight.
2. They couldn't maintain the weight loss—they soon started to gain again.

I came to the firm conclusion that a diet is not enough. It was necessary to develop and team a healthful lowered-calorie diet with a simple physical "action tool" and other support guides for peak concentration to keep the individual dieting, and then make the weight loss stick year after year.

Tested and used with patients in my office practice over a 16-year period to date, the result is my proved touch-control diet system. It will prove to you speedily that you too can slim down steadily, starting now, and then stay trim and enjoy a healthier life.

Perfecting the Diet

To coordinate with the touch-control action tool and supports, I recommended a balanced reducing diet to my patients, and planned eventually to create the most advanced and effective diet. Fortunately, I met Samm Sinclair Baker and have worked with him for over four years to get this book just right for you.

You will lose weight steadily on the DeBetz Diet because you will take in fewer calories than your body uses up. Thus, your system withdraws fat from your fat-storage areas, which developed and swelled due to overeating. Your weight drops, you firm up, bulges diminish and disappear. It's cause and effect, and you're the winner.

NOW YOU CONTROL YOUR EATING INSTEAD OF EATING CONTROLLING YOU

The discovery of the touch action to stop damaging eating habits came from my study of how overweight people eat. Usually they eat so automatically that the food takes control of them rather than controlling the intake themselves—and they don't even realize it! Nor do they know when they are truly hungry or when they've had enough. So they reach out for food at the wrong times.

To help overweight individuals get in touch with their feelings and bodies, I instructed them how to touch their faces as a reminder of their weight-loss goal. The physical touch became an instant stop signal to prevent overeating *before it began*. The touch worked.

Results were even more remarkable when the simple touch of finger on face was accompanied by three short STOPlines, which dieters repeated silently to themselves, taking less than 20 seconds. I added a vital SUPPORTlines procedure that strengthened the dieter even more. Proved with patient after patient, the diet-plus-touch combination stopped and replaced the long-standing habit of reaching out and eating rich, excessive food.

DIET PLUS TOUCH: WEIGHT LOSS BEGINS

You will learn in exact detail how the DeBetz Diet, coordinated with touch action, works so that you start losing unwanted weight right away, and then keeps lost pounds from sneaking back. You'll be focusing your emphasis on your healthier, more attractive body, and away from food, thus further erasing fat-eating habits (chapter 7). The lifelong stay-trim blueprint with easy, tested guidelines that have worked so well for my patients will help you keep your weight and figure in line thereafter.

Each day the "magic touch" keeps working for you as needed. As another happy dieter said, "It's touch and trim!" It's as dependable as this: You're about to enter a coffee shop for a weight-boosting high-calorie snack. Instead, you apply the touch action, which stops you instantly. You turn away instead of breaking your diet. It's as though a friend tapped you on the shoulder and reminded you not to indulge—so you don't.

Time after time, when eating a meal, you start to reach for a second portion or a diet-breaking pastry. Instead, you use the touch-control support in your fingertips to keep you trim for the rest of your life. This permanent touch-action support puts you in charge, so you'll never be heavy again.

This, too, is all-important. To make my two-way system work best, you must read every page of this book. Thus, you'll get the maximum benefits from the total reducing and weight-control program. Check the book again and again for needed refreshment and fortification—we all need reminders. Follow the simple instructions faithfully, and you too will say proudly, like my formerly overweight patients, "I'll never be heavy again."

Go to it, beginning today.

ESSENTIAL: YOUR DOCTOR'S APPROVAL

Before using this or any other diet, have a medical checkup, or phone for your doctor's approval. This requirement goes double if you have any health problems whatsoever or are pregnant—don't go on this or any other diet program without your physician's full permission. Only your physician can judge and advise for your individual condition, so don't take any chances.

2
YOUR TOUCH-CONTROL ACTION TOOL

Slims You Surely, Steadily, Keeps You Trim

Think of this as the first day of your slimmer life.

Please come into my office right now as, together, we begin your two-way reducing and permanent weight-control program via this book—which is your only "fee." Seat yourself comfortably. Feel confident that this is your new start, the innovative, proved help you've always needed to attain the slim, more attractive, and graceful body you want now and for the rest of your healthier life.

You can be certain of achieving your goal, since you'll grasp the easy-to-use touch-control directions in only a few minutes. Then you'll put them to use with the DeBetz Diet immediately. Unlike any other reducing program you've ever tried—which obviously failed you—now you'll combine our advanced diet with the action tool that keeps you dieting.

This two-way offensive—diet plus touch-control physical and emotional support—assures your steady weight loss until you reach your desired goal, and then will keep you trim lifelong. This double ammunition cannot fail to work for you as you work with it.

With touch-control, you'll possess the power of concentration. Having the ability to concentrate without strain will enhance your personal power to control your eating. That built-in mastery will enable you to overcome food temptation and never regain unwanted pounds.

TREATMENT AS AN OFFICE PATIENT

If you were my office patient, I would first take a general medical history, along with some basic tests. I would question you about your daily routines of personal care, food intake, and other pertinent matters. Once such details have been covered, I make sure permission has been given to you to diet by your own physician, which is essential, as I noted earlier.

As with every word in this book, I'm talking directly to you personally, to help you solve past overweight problems. I need your complete and dedicated cooperation, which you are eager to give. I'm delighted to be able to help you. Ready? Set? Let's lose weight.

HOW TO TOUCH AND LOSE WEIGHT

The first thing I want you to learn is touch-control, the wonderful aid that you've never had available to you before, so that you will finally succeed in slimming down. At last you can really look forward with full self-assurance. No more just dreaming about taking off unwanted pounds and inches; now you stop dreaming and start doing.

As assurance about how effectively this action tool can work for you, listen to a typical patient, Connie Thompson, age 29, a talented writer who lost 35 pounds with my methods: "Touch-control is the pause that reminds me, refreshes, renews, and strengthens my ability to resist temptation. It keeps me on your effective reducing diet as needed, and then keeps me slim. I've used your two-way touch-control system daily; it never fails me. Month after month, my weight stays the same, just where I want it. Now I'm sure that I'll never be heavy again."

You'll be acquiring both the two-way system and additional

ways that work—whys and hows in every chapter to make sure you take off excess weight day after day, and keep it off year after year. I'm going to help you become more aware and totally in touch with your body's needs—physically and emotionally— as you've never known how to up to now.

You're going to become a "thin eater" rather than the "fat eater" you were—yes, even if you're only a few pounds overweight. It's the "fat eating" that made you overweight, whether 5 or 50 pounds or more—and that's what you're going to be able to control. Again, you'll be in charge of your eating, instead of the eating being in charge of you.

That doesn't mean that you have to give up the enjoyment of delicious food and drink. Exactly the opposite; you can even have sparkling Champagne and wine on the DeBetz Diet, if you wish. As a "thin eater," you'll choose fine foods with discrimination, and you'll enjoy every bite. You won't stuff or gorge or swallow rich, fatty, high-calorie foodstuffs without thinking. The "magic touch" always at your fingertips will keep you from going overboard. One touch will interrupt and sidetrack undesirable eating and overeating.

How can a touch be such a lifesaver for you? Consider this comment by wise Samuel Johnson: "Depend on it, sir, when a man knows he's about to be hanged in a fortnight, it concentrates his mind wonderfully." You'll find that the touch concentrates your mind "wonderfully" on not eating that creamy lobster Newburg or other food loaded with fats and calories.

Think about this truth: Without personal control, without you being in charge of your eating, you often, even most of the time, eat although you're full and know you should stop. But all that will change from here on. Touch-control—including the supportive STOPlines you will learn shortly—will instill in you the thought that, for your body, overeating is an insult and a poison.

With the vital aid of touch-control, you'll keep reminding and convincing yourself that you need your body to live—and that you owe your body this respect and protection. Let it sink in: For your body, overeating is an insult and a poison. You're on your way to your slim-trim goal—not because I say so, but because your daily lower weight on the scale will prove it to you. The touch-control action tool will keep you in line as long and as often as you need it, right now and from now on.

Absolutely essential, the DeBetz Diet will be the basis of your daily eating from now until you are down to your desired weight. After you've reached your slim, trim goal, you'll go on to a wide variety of foods and menus of your choice, within the guidelines of the lifelong stay-trim blueprint (chapter 11). As never before, you'll find out how to analyze and consider foods before you eat—in short, how to eat to be slim and stay trim.

But first I want you to learn and make touch-control your own, your constant helpmate, guardian, and benefactor in your successful drive to reduce beautifully.

Simple Steps to Touch-Control Stop Action

You will make the "magic touch" part of your sure, successful daily reducing as simply as the directions here for your first practice session. You'll find that you touch and you're *connected*. Please follow through step by step now with these brief instructions. The entire touch-control procedure, which you'll use repeatedly, takes only 20 seconds.

Whenever you feel a strong urge or pressing desire to eat something that is not on your DeBetz Diet plan, instead of fighting it, admit it to yourself. At the same time, as you admit to the desire to eat, let's say, a piece of cake or pastry, also concentrate your mind on the commitment you have made to your body and yourself. Then do this (please practice this primary touch-control action right now): TOUCH ANY PART OF YOUR FACE GENTLY WITH THE TIP OF YOUR FOREFINGER. KEEP YOUR FINGERTIP THERE, TAKE A DEEP BREATH . . . AND THEN CONSIDER YOUR CHOICE.

Pause while touching, breathing deeply, concentrating on your commitment. Decide either to give in to the desire and eat that cake, thus insulting and poisoning your body—or to protect your body from the insult and injury that will result from eating that kind of damaging, diet-breaking food.

Now—fingertip touching your face, breathing deeply but comfortably—make your choice. Look again at that piece of cake (or the image of it), keep touching and concentrating—and the desire will dissipate. As soon as you touch, you'll feel the control difference. You'll be surprised and delighted that the urge to eat has passed. You'll feel proud that you held to your commitment.

Then remove your fingertip from your face. Now you know, having proved to yourself, that every time you look at tempting forbidden food, the touch-control fingertip signal will help you make the right choice for your body's health and beauty. You'll be strengthened by realizing that it's your choice, nobody else's. Each time your "won't eat it" power is intensified so that you'll make the right choice. The destructive desire to overindulge will pass. Your self-respect will grow. You'll feel very good about yourself.

I don't impose on you any rigid rules or restrictions about where you touch your face. Just reach out and touch gently wherever you feel provides the most comforting, most intimate contact. Your mouth zone—the area around and near your lips, even the lips themselves—is a natural, since that's where food enters as you eat. However, you may prefer to touch your chin, cheeks, forehead, ears, even your nose; some patients prefer to stroke an eyebrow. Try one spot, then another. Find out what is your personal best place to touch on your face.

Perhaps you'll enjoy touching the same spot each time because that seems to work best for you. Or touch a different area every time if you prefer variety. The prime purpose is to put you in touch with yourself—to put you in control of your eating from now on, to stop being a slave of food and eating.

Furthermore, you're not restricted to touching with your fingertip only. You may touch with several fingertips at once. Or touch with the side of a finger. The touching itself is what counts to make the needed connection. That signal activates the concentration process that keeps you from breaking your diet, keeps you losing weight.

Now you have an actual physical action tool to use to win through to your personal reducing and weight-control goals. Touch-control will work with you like any other effective tool designed to do a job—in this case, to take off excess pounds.

Pause . . . Reflect for a Moment

Plan to sit back a few times every day and reflect upon your ultimate goal, your slim, firm body. (In the next chapter I'll teach you the specific step-by-step support method that has worked so well for my patients.) In addition to these moments of private reflection, and visualizing your newly slimmed body, I want you to use the touch-control fingertip signal every time you are confronted with food.

I urge you to repeat the brief reflective pauses as part of the total system. They work for my patients—they will work for you. Accept that you have undoubtedly developed ingrained faulty food responses and bad eating and overeating habits over a long period of time. My instructions start you on a gradual corrective process that takes place in your brain as well as your body. What happens is that you are reprogramming your brain to carry through these two vital automatic functions smoothly and naturally:

1. To become intimately and constantly aware of your body and its needs.
2. To make the touch-control signal your own personal tool for reminding yourself of your commitment to your slim, more beautiful body and better health.

USING YOUR TOUCH-CONTROL SIGNAL

You'll be exceptionally pleased at how easy, pleasant, and natural it feels to use your touch-control signal. You just touch your face unselfconsciously as when thinking, reflecting, or simply relaxing; it's a common gesture. You can get the benefits from the touch-action tool anytime anywhere without anyone noticing or knowing what you're doing. For instance, you'll touch:

■ At meals at home or at a friend's to stop yourself from eating rich food or from taking an extra serving that will ruin your diet.

■ In a restaurant to make sure that you make the right choice from the menu, not breaking your diet.

■ At a party to keep from giving in to the automatic response of grabbing those high-calorie nuts and hors d'oeuvres just because they are sitting there or are offered to you.

■ At those times when you may feel irritated, bored, angry, or otherwise frustrated, and would ordinarily just reach out for taboo calorie-adding food without thinking about it.

From now on, instead of munching, gulping, gorging mindlessly and harmfully, you will use the touch-control signal that you just practiced briefly: *Touch . . . deep breath . . . concentrate . . .* and the desire evaporates. It works—you'll avoid eating at those inappropriate times.

I urge you to read every word of the preceding pages in this chapter again, slowly. Let each directive sink in deeply. Repeat the practice instructions. Having done that, you're now ready to learn the touch-control 20-second shape-up with the three proved powerful STOPlines. You'll be using the instant routine as a brake to stop you from ever breaking your diet. You'll find it as simple and effective as applying the brake to stop a speeding car.

TOUCH-CONTROL 20-SECOND STOPPER

I'll explain how and why each step works right after you read and practice the quickie routine. What's all-important to you, beyond any explanation, is that it works. Do this now:

1. Look upward, then quickly close your eyes. (Time, two seconds.)
2. Touch your face gently with the tip of your forefinger (anywhere on your face).
3. Repeat these three STOPlines to yourself:

For my body, overeating is an insult and a poison.
I need my body to live.
I owe my body this respect and attention.

Take 20 seconds now to perform this total touch-control stop routine. Pause and take a few deep breaths. Perform the procedure again. Pause once more and take a few deep breaths. Repeat the 20-second stopper a third time. You found the short session relaxing, refreshing, and bolstering—right?

This stopper process works so well because it wasn't just originated or snatched out of midair haphazardly. I developed and perfected the routine during my medical training and practice with overweight patients over the years. It worked to enable them to lose pounds steadily until down to their desired weight —and to stay trim year after year. Proved by these delighted slimmed-down women and men, the entire touch-control process will work for you. It will repeatedly divert your attention from food and put you back in touch with your commitment to reduce.

How and Why Each Step Works

Looking upward is a natural automatic concentration action used by people everywhere. Usually you're not even aware of doing it. Consider how often you have done this yourself: You're seeking a solution to a problem—you find that you look upward unconsciously in order to concentrate best. Someone asks you a question that requires a thoughtful answer. You look upward as you frame your most fitting response, then you answer. You're filling out a questionnaire or you're taking a test: You look upward automatically, without even realizing it, in order to concentrate on thinking through and selecting the most accurate answer.

The next time you watch a TV talk show, notice that when the interviewer asks a probing question, the interviewee almost always looks upward. He (or she) fixes his gaze on an invisible spot on the ceiling as he ponders his answer and concentrates on choosing the most meaningful words. As Emerson wrote, "Concentration is the secret of strength . . . in all management of human affairs." In this case, your concentration is on managing your weight with the active aid of touch-control procedures.

The natural, automatic physical movement of looking upward at a fixed spot, or just at the ceiling or sky, even for a second or two, sharpens your focus. With eyes up, you think for a few seconds—and you withdraw from the act of eating. You skip the excess calorie-laden food, and you keep taking off pounds.

Touching your face with your fingertip—at the same time as you look upward and close your eyes—is the basic physical alerting signal to yourself to take special notice. The tingling, intimate warmth of skin against skin is a penetrating cue to reject temptation decisively. You keep dieting and losing weight.

Now, with eyes closed and concentration total, you silently repeat and activate your consciousness with the first powerful STOPline:

For my body, overeating is an insult and a poison.

Focusing forcefully on the grim truth of that stopper sentence helps you understand convincingly the necessity of continuing positive action to prevent overeating *at that instant*. You determine to shove the seductive food aside as you remind yourself that it's destructive to your health, your appearance, your total well-being. For further reinforcement, you repeat the second STOPline:

I need my body to live.

This repeated emphasis sharpens your awareness of the serious threat in being overweight. It is the beginning of your all-important shifting of gears—away from the lure of food to incalculable benefits for your body. This needed physical and mental pinpointing starts the wonderful constructive change in your life-style from fat and flabby to trim and firm. (You'll get more detailed how-to directions in chapter 7.) Now to the third STOPline:

I owe my body this respect and attention.

This STOPline underscores your personal responsibility to improve and sustain your body at its best. I know that you care deeply about achieving maximum health and slenderness, or you wouldn't be reading this book. Repeating this STOPline and the others, along with the entire 20-second touch action, will enable you—as you never could before—to resist diet-breaking food and to keep losing those unwanted pounds and inches.

You don't fall off your diet. A gratified, newly slim patient called this "the touch of self-respect."

You'll find that you obtain an extra benefit, as using the three STOPlines functions to shift emphasis from the food to your desired body image. With every pound lost, your healthier, more attractive body assumes greater importance and delights you increasingly.

Summing it up, the more you use the touch-action tool, the more you keep dieting and losing burdensome excess pounds, surely, steadily, healthfully.

STOP SIGNAL STOPPED DAY-AND-NIGHT SNACKING

Here's exactly how the stop signal worked superbly for Joan Brosfeld, 52, a customer aide in a large bank. In her words, "Reducing with touch-control saved my job. Going through divorce, my weight shot up to 168 pounds. I looked massive and clumsy, felt terrible. I tried diets, lost a few pounds, gained them right back again. I was a human yo-yo.

"My biggest problem was snacking during the day and in the lonely nights. At coffee breaks morning and afternoon, I couldn't resist rich doughnuts and pastries. Getting up once or twice nightly to go to the bathroom, I'd raid the refrigerator. I couldn't stop myself until I learned your touch-control system. Frankly, I was doubtful before I started, but it works like magic for me.

"Since I was so overweight, your diet took off pounds amazingly fast and steadily. The stop signal blocked me every time I'd start to reach for a fattening snack. At night I'd open the refrigerator, pause to use the 20-second stopper—then close the door. The stopper is a lifesaver for me!

"Now, for months, I've been down to 135 pounds, my goal, 33 pounds lighter. People at work tell me I look great. You wouldn't believe my social life—it's thrilling."

Night eating and high-calorie snacking at any time are common overweight problems. The touch-control stop signal is particularly effective in getting you to pause and concentrate for 20 seconds—then you pull your hand back, saved by the touch. You'll find out for yourself.

PRACTICE 20-SECOND TOUCH ACTION NOW

I have taken you through the simple 20-second touch-action procedure in this chapter step by step—just as I've done innumerable times with my patients, who then succeeded happily in reducing and keeping trim. As I instructed them to do, I want you to practice the pleasant routine repeatedly now before coordinating the touch-action process with the DeBetz Diet. Thus, you'll score sure weight loss from the first day.

Reread this entire chapter carefully to make this touch-control stop process part of your daily program. Remember that with a touch—more effective each time you apply it—you control undesirable eating and overeating, preventing the eating from controlling you.

Then, just as easy to learn in only minutes, go on to attain the touch-control support procedure. Strengthening the forceful stop effect even more, you'll benefit from this extension of touch-control immediately and for the rest of your life.

Using both the stop and support processes, teamed with the DeBetz Diet, you'll find yourself feeling secure about your ultimate weight-loss and weight-control success. The next chapter will supply the second part of the reinforced touch-control power you need as you coordinate with the specific diet that follows immediately after. It adds up, your power multiplying with each step: Touch plus diet will be your personal two-way success formula.

3
YOUR TOUCH-CONTROL SUPPORT BOOST
Keeps You from Gaining Weight Year After Year

Backing up the DeBetz Diet with the touch-control action tool and STOPlines has been exceptionally successful in helping overweight patients take off excess pounds. "Time after time," said patient Carl Podello, 52, an airline dispatcher who took off 23 excess pounds, "the stop action worked as though another hand held mine back from reaching for an extra portion of mashed potatoes and gravy. Then, as I slimmed down and felt great about it, I stopped reaching. I just didn't want high-calorie gook any more. Your peak concentration technique keeps me trim. It's terrific!"

The procedure worked for Carl Podello in his high-pressure job and can for you—just as surely as if a friend were standing by always to block your thrusting hand and pull you back from gorging on something like a double-dipped chocolate ice-cream bar. The touch and STOPlines are always as close as your fingertips to help stop you from excessive eating any minute of the day and night.

Reducing results were excellent for patient after patient, but I was wary. I knew from my extensive medical and psychiatric experience that bad eating habits are usually deeply ingrained. They must be changed for good, not temporarily modified— lest they keep coming back.

I determined, out of necessity, to develop a backup system, a support strategy that would strengthen and provide a deep-rooted, more permanent barrier to prevent the overweight individual from becoming careless and then falling off the diet. What to do about it to assure continued weight loss?

Treating overweight patients and following their progress in detail week after week, I developed what was needed. I added a second support sequence to the stop procedure, which has already been taught to you. That's what you're going to acquire now, a backup system that provides *double protection* against yielding to temptation and regaining lost pounds.

Is such a second support system really necessary? No question about it, even though other programs have bypassed this need up to now. It was clear to me from data amassed during all the years of working with overweight people that bolstering the dieter's resolve was not only desirable but absolutely essential in the overwhelming majority of cases. Personal control by the dieter had to be ever-present not only while dieting but also to maintain trimness and better health, once achieved (note details of your lifelong stay-trim blueprint in chapter 11).

Many patients who had lost some weight on other diet programs, and then gained it back and more, complained that once they came off those diets they had a sense of being lost. They didn't know what to do next, and that drove them back into their old fat eating and overeating habits. That won't happen to you with my support methods and guidelines.

An extreme example of feeling lost through lack of support is a patient, Henrietta Gold, 36, a restaurant hostess. The doctor who referred her to me mentioned her long history of weight problems. She had recently lost weight too rapidly on a severely limited diet. She was so frightened of gaining it back that she stopped eating almost entirely. She told me, "I dropped 85 pounds because I wanted enough leeway in case I started gaining again. I was worried sick, and a good friend insisted that I see you."

Clearly, Mrs. Gold was overwhelmed by fears of becoming overweight again, as you'll note from a dream she related to me (perhaps you've had similar nightmares): "In my dream I was driving a car over a long bridge. As I approached the end of the bridge I saw that it had collapsed ahead of me. I was panicked about falling off into the gushing water below. I stamped on the car brake and stopped just before I'd crash off the bridge. I woke up in a cold sweat, trembling and anxious."

After she calmed down and answered some questions, I interpreted the dream for her: "I think your dream paralleled what you'd just gone through; you're worried about going through it again. Look at it this way: In the dream you came from one direction, that is, your old eating habits. The bridge became the period of losing weight." She was paying very close attention.

I continued, "Approaching the other end of the bridge, you were coming to a new highway, that is, your new eating habits. Your past weight-reduction experiences brought you only through the middle of the bridge, then almost to the end—but you didn't know any way to go from there except to tumble all the way down, back to your old eating habits." She nodded in agreement.

I went on, "But this time it's different. There's no reason to be frightened. The 'bridge,' my support methods, will get you over to a new road, your new eating habits. And, knowing you're strongly supported, you'll be able to drive that road straight ahead with full confidence. Your two-way touch-control system will be there waiting to work for you and with you, once you have crossed the bridge, that is, reached your ideal body weight."

Her smile of understanding had wiped the worry from her face. You'll feel the same confidence with the support you'll have, which everyone should be given when dieting and after losing excess weight.

THE NEW BACKUP SUPPORT SYSTEM EMERGES

Through testing and repeated checking with a large variety of patients, I developed new ideas from which the needed successful backup support system emerged to counter both physical and emotional pressures. The innovative procedure proved effective with a succession of women and men of varying types and ages. They not only reduced, but stayed trim year after year.

There was no longer any question: The new support system worked marvelously. As you'll learn, the backup support technique incorporated three SUPPORTlines. The support system teamed most effectively with the stop process and its three STOPlines, each procedure strengthening the other. The combination, coordinated with the DeBetz Diet, will help you take off excess weight steadily and healthfully, starting from day one of your diet.

You'll find the SUPPORTlines just as easy to use as the basic touch-control method you've practiced already. They will give you confidence in your ultimate reducing success. That self-assurance is vital as you prepare to start the diet that follows in the next chapter. You'll begin enjoying a new uplift of energy and well-being, along with pride in a better-looking body.

LEARNING THE TOUCH-CONTROL SUPPORT BOOST

With the SUPPORTlines, you will use the same touch-control action as with the STOPlines, which you will continue to apply as needed. Use the stop action tool as often as required, to keep yourself from yielding to every temptation that might arise to break your diet.

To supplement that stop-action use, you'll employ the support boost five to ten times daily. You can perform the simple procedure either sitting, standing, or lying down, whichever is convenient. You may utilize this SUPPORTlines touch system upon awakening, at bedtime, anytime. You'll find all the brief sessions pleasurable and sustaining, your motivation to keep going. The peak concentration you experience is refreshing and energizing.

Please practice the primary touch-control action again right now as a refresher, even though you may know it well from past application:

Touch any part of your face gently with the tip of your forefinger. Keeping your fingertip there, take a deep breath . . . and concentrate for a few seconds on affirming your commitment to lose your excess weight. Let out your breath. Remove your fingertip. Now relax and absorb the following augmented directions for your support boost:

1. Look up, then close your eyes.
2. Touch your face with a relaxed finger.
3. Visualize your overweight body as if viewing it in a full-length mirror. Then zoom in on your stomach in close-up. Now, using the three forceful, proved SUPPORTlines, ask yourself silently:

> *How hungry am I right now?*
> *How much have I eaten so far today?*
> *What am I going to eat the rest of the day?*

Pause after asking yourself each question to consider and then answer honestly, no self-deception.
4. Then, eyes closed, still using your visual imagination, take your time to scan your naked body critically, inch by inch, as if seen on a video screen inside your head. Don't spare yourself. Keep examining slowly, analytically, with ruthless candor—regardless of how much you may disapprove of what you see. It's vital not to hide from yourself.
5. Then *change the picture!* Concentrate on seeing your slimmed, desired body image in your mind's mirror—and also think of your new trim contours winning admiration in the eyes of others. Delight in the vision of your trimmer, healthier, more graceful body as you will see and enjoy it at rest and in motion. Tell yourself emphatically: *"This is my positive goal. This is how I'm going to look and feel. Now I know that I'll never be heavy again."* Take time to enjoy your vision of the "new you" fully.
6. Remove your hand so that your fingertip no longer touches your face. Then open your eyes and feel thoroughly relaxed.

Practice the support boost a few times to get it right, to help it sink in deeply. The effectiveness of the pleasant exercise will increase each time you use the procedure. The result will be to solidify your determination to finally slim down and stay trim.

By following the DeBetz Diet each day—turning off temptations that are bound to arise—you will lose weight steadily. You will be aided constantly by using the touch-control stop action as needed. You will be strengthening your resolve and ability to keep dieting and taking off unwanted pounds and inches as you practice the backup touch-control support procedure several times daily. You'll change from having been a fat eater to naturally enjoying being a thin eater from now on and lifelong.

UNDERSTANDING AND OVERCOMING THE DELUSION OF "HUNGER"

What is your reducing goal? To lose 10 pounds, 20 pounds, 30 pounds or more? Whatever your target of desired weight, you can reach it now with my instructions, as you become what I refer to as a "thin eater." As such, you will understand what true hunger is, and then you will overcome the destructive delusion of hunger.

I call it delusion of hunger because you probably have very rarely experienced true hunger. I want you to be aware of a common confusion about hunger versus appetite that I've seen in many patients: Hunger is a physiological (physical) sensation, while appetite is a psychological desire for food, triggered by a variety of factors such as sight, smell, or even the mere thought of a particular food.

An easy way to differentiate between hunger and appetite is that appetite is usually for a specific food, while hunger is a vague gnawing sensation in the pit of your stomach. Think about this as a reminder the next time you think you're hungry.

Take the time now to digest the truth about hunger. Concentrate on making this truth an integral part of your overcoming bad eating habits and overeating. You start to become a thin eater as you ask yourself the first SUPPORTline, "How hungry am I right now?"—and learn to answer with complete honesty. As a thin eater, you will not be deceived by the delusion of false hunger, you will look at food for what it is: nutrition for your body.

Once you use food as something else, merely as further intake, as in stuffing your mouth and body greedily, it becomes an insult and poison for your body. As a thin eater, aided by touch-control action and support, you will be in constant touch with your body's needs for good health and well-being—which over-weight acts to destroy. You will eat when you are truly hungry, and stop as soon as the body has had enough for its needs.

You, however—and the proof is your being overweight—have lost touch with the true physical sensations of hunger. Many times you eat without being hungry. And you usually overeat although your body told you when to stop because it felt full. That's true, isn't it? Of course you admit it, since you no longer will hide the truth from yourself.

You have made the decision to lose your overweight and keep it off permanently. Therefore, you are making firm com-mitments to yourself. One of those commitments is summed up in the STOPlines you've learned and adopted. Review those commitments now:

For my body, overeating is an insult and a poison.
I need my body to live.
I owe my body this respect and attention.

Imbued with your commitments, as summed up in the STOP-lines, you are on your way to becoming a thin eater and a slim person for the rest of your better life. You will start today on the DeBetz Diet. From this day on, while following the diet and afterward, you will base every eating experience on a sensible judgment about food. You will abolish the impulsive, unthink-ing, often damaging food intake that made you overweight in the past.

HOW THE SUPPORTLINES WORK FOR YOU

You will be able to accomplish the all-important transition from fat eater to thin eater not because I say so but for this fundamental reason: From now on, before you eat—whether a snack or a meal—it will be an ingrained step for you to repeat the touch-control support sequence before you put any food in your body.

Right now, as though you were about to gobble a favorite dish, perhaps a slice of hot double-cheese pizza, do this immediately: Touch your face . . . look upward for deep concentration . . . close your eyes . . . repeat to yourself silently and thoughtfully the three SUPPORTlines:

How hungry am I right now?
How much have I eaten so far today?
What am I going to eat the rest of the day?

After you have taken a few seconds to ask and answer the questions clearly, open your eyes. Look at the food, imaginary or real, for 10 to 15 seconds as you consider whether you are *really* hungry or not right now. Then ask yourself these two simple questions:

"Is this food I am about to eat the right food for me in its quality and amount?"

"Does this food comply with the DeBetz Diet, to which I have committed myself?"

If the answer to both questions is "yes," then go ahead and eat with pleasure. Enjoy every mouthful slowly, chewing thoroughly.

If, however, the answer to both questions is "no," then take the food and put it back where it belongs; return it to the refrigerator or cupboard. Or even dump it into the garbage can—not into your body! Keep in the forefront of your consciousness that your body is your precious instrument for living. It is your personal and sole responsibility to protect your body and health from the harm of fat eating and overeating.

Like practically all the overweight women and men I have helped, you usually take your body for granted. There is you, the individual, and somehow there is a body attached. It's an unfortunate fact that usually we don't think too much about the constant care required by our bodies until something goes wrong. That's true of you, isn't it?

But from now on your attitude is changed. You are committed to eating "healthy" and taking off your unhealthy overweight.

Before drastic physical and perhaps psychological damage occurs, you have decided definitely that the time to lose your overweight is now. Following that up, you are determined to maintain your desired body weight lifelong.

Remember always, therefore, before you eat anything, to use your touch-control stop action before reaching for a diet-breaking temptation—and apply the support procedure before choosing and eating any food. For extra support, touch not only your mouth area, but also your forehead, and finally your stomach. All three actions help focus your peak concentration on losing weight. Then ask yourself the questions embodied in the three SUPPORT lines.

Every time you touch yourself this way, you will feel the supportive difference as you remind yourself to stop long enough to assess correctly whether the eating in each instance is indicated or not. In this way, again, you put increasing emphasis on your body. The effect is that food and the act of eating become far less important in your daily life. Each day the transformation escalates into your being an established thin eater—replacing permanently the fat eater you were in the past.

You become more and more confident as you use the touch-control signals as your tools to develop and build your sense of self-discipline and firm control. Each touch builds a barrier to prevent picking up and eating thickly buttered rolls, pastries, other diet-breaking food. You will be thrilled and supported always by the self-assurance that you are in control of what you eat—that the food does not control you any longer.

Now—knowing and using both touch-control stop and support procedures—you are ready to coordinate them with the DeBetz Diet. You begin the diet with firm confidence that this time you will succeed, as you were never able to before.

4

THE TOUCH-CONTROL DAY-BY-DAY DIET

For the first time in your life, probably, you'll be starting a healthful reducing diet with full self-confidence that you'll lose excess pounds day by day until you're down to your desired weight. You have that self-assurance because you know by now that the 20-second stop procedure will keep you from falling off the satisfying DeBetz Diet.

And that basic, fortifying conviction is backed by the knowledge that you'll have *double* reinforcement this time: The repeated support boost will keep you dieting confidently day after day until you're just as slim as you want to be. Once you have reached your goal, use the stop and support systems you've learned in preceding pages, along with a dependable, clear blueprint to follow to stay trim lifelong. No other diet program has ever provided such unique, easy-to-use methods that work.

In summary, I emphasize again that you can count on not just an effective diet that will take off up to five or more pounds a week but also the first diet coordinated with touch-control. With that combination, you can slim down and stay trim, no matter how often you may have failed before.

A newly slim patient, Diane Eldridge, 28, a laboratory technician, said, "I started losing weight from the first day on your diet with its amazing simplicity. The eating satisfied me, and I never felt hungry or tired. Your support systems kept me going without faltering. I felt vigorous and healthy all the way. Your program sure gave me nutritional security that will help me stay healthier and thin."

Your "nutritional security" is backed by the protein-fat-carbohydrate balance of the DeBetz Diet: 33 percent protein (primarily from poultry, fish, and shellfish rather than red meat), 16 percent fat (very low, but definitely sufficient), and 51 percent complex carbohydrates (almost entirely from vegetables, fruits, fiber—not sugars and starches). The diet provides vitamins and minerals, including calcium and other valuable elements, in moderation.

The excellent nutritional composition of the diet was double-checked in detail through a sophisticated computer analysis by the authoritative American Health Foundation, Nutrition Department, under the supervision of nutritionist Carol Cohen.

This balance accords with latest scientific findings and recommendations for most healthful eating. Included in my development of the diet are findings of the landmark National Academy of Sciences report on diet, nutrition, and cancer, as well as a recent Boston symposium on nutrition under the auspices of the Harvard Medical School. The conclusions of research by other professionally recognized sources are combined in the evolution of the diet you will be following.

"AMAZING SIMPLICITY"

Right from the start I knew that, to be effective, any diet has to be simple, so simplicity is a notable feature of my diet. No counting calories. No weighing portions. Just follow faithfully the daily listings and the few sensible "must" guidelines.

There's no complicated food preparation involved. You'll find good, clean healthful eating that everyone can enjoy, dieting or not. Some delicious creative pilot recipes are given in the next chapter as general guides for those who like to cook. But you don't have to do any specialized cooking. The diet is simple and satisfying for eating in or eating out. You cook your own way or order in restaurants. Just stay within the basic guidelines provided.

You will certainly not be on this diet forever—only during a limited period until you're down to your desired weight. Then you'll eat what you enjoy most from a large variety of foods, as noted in the lifelong stay-trim blueprint provided for you later. The stop and support systems that will have become ingrained in you—along with the five-pound "return" signal—will prevent you from zooming up in weight.

CHECK YOUR WEIGHT DAILY

I want you to weigh yourself every morning while on the diet —and at regular intervals after that. If you're afraid to step on the scale any day, that usually means you think you've eaten too much and gained some pounds—and want to hide that fact from yourself. Of course, you must be honest with yourself in order to reach your goal.

So if you are ever reluctant to step on the scale and face the music, take 20 seconds for a calming stop sequence. Repeat the reminder STOPlines. You'll feel refreshed and reinforced instantly. Remember that the all-important repeated help of the stop and support boosts is at your fingertips always.

Welcome the assistance of your scale as your monitor, your faithful guardian pointing out daily how you're doing. Seeing your weight drop steadily on the scale is the greatest encouragement. If the numbers don't go down, recheck the diet guidelines to see what you're not doing or are doing wrong. You just can't help but slim down on this diet unless you're indulging in rich, diet-breaking eating or overeating.

If you're not losing pounds steadily, ask yourself, "Am I adhering to the instructions accurately?" Review in your mind exactly what you ate the day before and whether you were active or have hardly been using your body at all (see chapter 10 on activity pointers and recommendations). Follow the easy-to-understand directions, and your weight must and will go down as you trim off those unwanted excess inches.

Consider the scale as your dependable watchdog—if the number goes up, the signal is as clear as an angry growl. The scale need not be complex or costly. With the numbers right there in sight, you don't have to guess at "How'm I doing?" The scale won't flatter or lie to you, as a relative or well-meaning friend might.

Just get on the scale unclothed first thing each morning, before eating. Otherwise, the size of your breakfast, and the amount and type of clothing you're wearing, can distort your true weight. Your food and clothing vary some from day to day, right?

You'll find it helpful and very desirable to jot down your weight while on the diet—using a chart such as the one on page 35. Just write your weight in the blank space each day. After you're down to your desired weight and on stay-trim maintenance eating, weighing yourself two or three times a week is usually sufficient. Of course, you can continue to get on the scale each morning if you like.

On the following page is a "Desirable Weight Chart" for you to study as a guide. Pick the number that specifies your desired weight according to the instructions, then go to it.

DESIRABLE WEIGHT CHART

Weigh yourself upon arising, before eating, unclothed. Consider these numbers as a general guide. Since individuals differ, the weights based on gender and height provide a wide range. The figures are derived from a variety of medical tables, patient experience, and life insurance company tabulations. Select your most desirable weight according to how you look and feel best, checking with what your physician recommends as best for you.

I purposely don't break down the weight ranges according to age or "small, medium, large frame." It has been my experience that most overweight people, when given that choice, tend to select the "large frame" number as permitting them to weigh at the heaviest rather than the healthiest figure. I stress again that you should consult with your doctor about what weight is most healthful, physically and emotionally, for you individually.

Height	Women Range in Lbs.	Men Range in Lbs.
4'8"	88–96	96–102
4'9"	90–98	98–105
4'10"	92–100	99–108
4'11"	94–104	100–109
5'	96–106	104–114
5'1"	98–110	106–120
5'2"	102–115	112–125
5'3"	107–120	117–132
5'4"	112–125	122–138
5'5"	115–129	126–142
5'6"	120–134	132–147
5'7"	122–138	137–150
5'8"	127–145	140–156
5'9"	132–147	146–162
5'10"	137–150	152–166
5'11"	142–156	157–172
6'	146–160	160–177
6'1"		166–185
6'2"		172–190
6'3"		177–195
6'4"		182–200
6'5"		187–205

With this day-by-day, week-by-week record, you can see on any day exactly how much you weighed on the same day of the week or weeks before, and any other day, week by week. You can even see at a glance your weight loss for a full month. You'll feel cheered as you review your steady progress to your goal: the slimmed, attractive figure you had visualized repeatedly during your touch-control support sessions.

Depending on how many pounds you wish to lose, you may reach your desired weight goal in a week or two. Or, if you have a good many pounds to lose, it may take you longer than four weeks. In the latter case, you'll be delighted that you're losing steadily, and you'll keep going, sustained always by the daily stop and support procedures. Make an additional chart, and

YOUR WEIGHT-LOSS RECORD
Day by Day, Week by Week

NAME _____   DATE _____

WEIGHT AT START _____ lbs.   DESIRED WEIGHT GOAL _____ lbs.

	Mon.	Tues.	Wed.	Thurs.	Fri.	Sat.	Sun.
1st week							
2nd week							
3rd week							
4th week							

continue recording your weight loss daily until you reach your goal.

Of course, you need not start your dieting on a Monday. Whatever day of the week you begin your DeBetz Diet, fill in the number of pounds, and go on losing from there until you reach your goal.

As an example of how to fill in your chart, here's a typical record of a patient, Linda Carolla, age 42, 5'3", a determined English teacher. She told me at the start, "When I was 25 years old, I weighed 120 pounds and was repeatedly complimented on my beautiful figure, even if I say so myself. At age 30, my weight had crept up to 130 pounds. I tried a diet but by age 35 I weighed 137 pounds, and the compliments had stopped.

"I failed to reduce on diet after diet—I just couldn't stick to any of them. The pounds kept piling on. This morning I topped 138 pounds on the scale. I was shocked that I had come close to 140. My clothes don't fit, I hate my looks in the mirror. I'm envious of a relative who trimmed down beautifully with your methods. She suggested that I see you. I'm dying to get back to the figure I was so proud of when I was 25. I hope you can help me, but I'm doubtful. I've failed so often."

Linda Carolla calls me early every January to wish me "Happy New Year." Recently, three years after she first came to see me, she phoned and announced triumphantly, "I'm still only 120 pounds and holding. I feel marvelous, especially since my husband and friends keep complimenting me on my trim figure. I go back on the diet and touch-control now and then, and they sure work."

NAME Linda Carolla   DATE Jan. 4

WEIGHT AT START 138 lbs.   DESIRED WEIGHT GOAL 120 lbs.

	Mon.	Tues.	Wed.	Thurs.	Fri.	Sat.	Sun.
1st week	138	136	134	133	132	131	130
2nd week	130	129	128	128	127	127	126
3rd week	126	125	125	124	124	123	123
4th week	123	122	122	121	121	121	120

10 "MUST" GUIDELINES

Just observe these 10 "must" guidelines every day while on the DeBetz Diet and you'll lose pounds steadily, right down to your desired weight goal:

1. Use the stop touch-control procedure along with the STOPlines wherever and whenever you are tempted to eat diet-breaking snacks or servings, or to overeat. Before you pick up that buttersoaked English muffin, touch . . . and you'll desist. Never put off or skip this sure stopping power.

2. Keep strengthening your exact adherence to the diet by repeating the touch-control sustaining process with the SUPPORTlines five to ten times daily during your waking hours.

3. Follow the daily diet listings every day, as shown. Don't make any substitutions and don't deviate unless permitted in the detailed instructions that follow the week's day-by-day listings. If you don't know whether or not a certain food is permitted, don't eat it—pass it by. A doubtful choice is usually the wrong choice.

4. Eat moderate portions only. I know that you can't weigh or measure every serving—that wouldn't be practicable or make good sense. In general, a "moderate" portion of chicken or fish is about 6 ounces, most meats about 4 ounces, vegetables 1 cup, cereals 1 cup.

By observing the daily food listings, you will be consuming between 900 and 1,200 calories a day. You're an individual human being with individual differences, so no one can honestly say precisely that you will be eating 921 or 1,057 or 1,196½ calories a day. The total calories you take in will vary according to the size of the portions you choose to consume.

Since most overweight women and men usually consume between 2,500 and 10,000 or more calories a day (a shocking number but too true), it's clear that you'll lose up to five pounds or considerably more a week, depending on how overweight you are, how many calories you ate on average before going on the diet, and how careful and accurate you are in dieting daily.

Whether you choose small portions and thus consume 900 to 1,000 calories daily, or select moderate portions, as directed while on the diet according to the daily listing, you'll be eating about 1,000 to 1,100 calories daily. The 1,200-calorie top figure encompasses some leeway, but I urge you to adhere to moderate or even small portions in order to lose pounds surely and steadily.

5. Don't drink any high-calorie beverages. You may enjoy coffee and tea, hot or iced, preferably decaffeinated—no cream or milk or sugar added. You may sweeten drinks with sugar substitute if desired, in moderation. You may have sugar-free carbonated beverages in a variety of flavors, in moderation (don't overdo anything). Drink plenty of water. While milk is a healthful beverage, drink only the amounts that appear in the daily listings, then have milk and milk products in moderation after you're down to your desired weight. You'll learn to enjoy skim or low-fat milk instead of whole milk.

Beverage listing at meals (and anytime you want a beverage between meals) includes hot or iced coffee, tea (preferably decaffeinated), sugar-free sodas in your choice of flavors, salt- and sugar-free club soda, seltzer, naturally carbonated water—and, of course, plain water, as many glasses as you can drink comfortably per day.

Sparkling Beverage Bonus: Enjoy a 3-ounce glass of dry Champagne for lunch or dinner—or any dry sparkling wine (imported or domestic), or any still dry light wine, white or red —if you like an alcoholic wine to sparkle up a meal. Also, you may mix 3 ounces of dry white or red wine with seltzer or club soda in a large glass for a sparkling drink called a "spritzer." But caution: only one glass per day.

Don't drink any other alcoholic beverages while you're on the diet—you'll be able to drink moderately, if you wish, when you're trim and shift to the stay-trim eating blueprint. To add sparkle without any alcohol at a meal or between meals, have a glass or more of seltzer or sugar-free soda in your favorite flavors.

THE CHAMPAGNE DIET

Some of my formerly overweight patients so enjoyed the suggested daily sparkling drink, along with the good food on the diet, that they call this the "Champagne Diet." A daily glass of dry Champagne (or other sparkling or dry wine, or non-alcoholic, sugar-free carbonated beverage) can be a gastronomical and psychological lift. In a welcome new development, an "ultra-brut, sans-dosage" Champagne, under 25 calories per ounce, entirely sugar-free, is becoming available in various brands nationwide.

You can skip the sparkling, drink, Champagne or otherwise, if you wish—it's not a must.

A newly slim patient, Arnold E. Halversen, 61, member of a leading gourmet society, told me after he'd reached his goal by losing 23 pounds, "Your Champagne Diet is not only extraordinarily effective, but also it's the first *civilized* diet I've known. I looked forward to the sparkling lift at the end of each day—it added greatly to my pleasure in becoming vigorously trim again."

The French Champagne producers insist that if the product doesn't come from the Champagne district of France, it's not true Champagne. They cite health benefits in drinking Champagne in moderation, and are proud that Konrad Adenauer, famed Chancellor of West Germany, among others, imbibed Champagne regularly until he died at age 91. In any case, whether or not you have a daily glass of Champagne or another sparkling, my toast to you is "*À votre santé*"—to your health.

6. Don't use fats in cooking, food preparation, or as additives —no butter or margarine (same calories as butter), no oils, mayonnaise, rich dressings of any kind. No butter or margarine for spreading or melting. No oils on salads. If desired, you may use dressings, bottled or homemade, that have no more than 16 calories per tablespoon—but lemon juice and vinegars are preferable. Also, note the delicious very-low-calorie dressing recipes in chapters 5 and 6.

For cooking, in many cases you can use a little nonstick vegetable cooking spray. You may use lemon juice and vinegars, and in cooking a little wine is permitted, since the alcohol calories burn away in the heat processing and only the flavor and moistness are added. You'll find that fine foods can be more healthful, and with clean, delicious natural flavor, when you eliminate added fats.

7. Remove all visible fat from any servings before preparing and eating. Always remove skin and visible fat from chicken and turkey. Select lean meats only, and remove all visible fat. Avoid the fatty types of fish (see special listings and detailed calorie content listings in chapter 12).

8. Vegetables aplenty, high in vitamins and minerals, are listed for lunches and dinners daily. Flavor them to your taste with seasonings and spices, lemon juice, and very little salt or preferably no added salt. Don't add any fats at all, no butter, margarine, oils. Again, let the true fresh natural flavors come through. You'll find them much more tasty that way, and far better for you, a great aid in slimming and staying trim.

Fruits are to be eaten only according to the daily diet listings, and never with sugar added. Nor should calorie-rich syrups be present or added.

9. Between meals, use the 20-second stop action as often as needed to prevent breaking your diet with high-calorie prohibited foods as snacks.

10. Here are some enjoyable low-calorie snacks to savor between meals if wanted:

Drink low-calorie, low-sodium consommé and broth (under 13 calories per cup); you may add favorite seasonings to tune up the taste. A cup of fat-free hot broth at almost any time is filling and delicious.

Munch raw vegetables prepared ahead of time and kept readily at hand in the refrigerator; also you can carry some to work in a plastic bag or other container. Don't limit yourself to a few types. The excellent variety available includes celery strips, sweet pepper slices, mushroom shavings, carrot sticks, cherry tomatoes, radishes, asparagus tips, broccoli and cauliflower florets, zucchini pieces, cucumber segments, watercress, alfalfa sprouts, other raw vegetables that you like. In addition to the vegetables, you may enjoy moderate amounts of popcorn, no salt or fats added.

You can make raw vegetables even more savory with a sprinkle or marinade of fresh lemon juice, vinegar, seasonings, spices.

Delight in several servings a day, if you like, of sugar-free gelatin desserts in a range of delicious flavors.

THE DAY-BY-DAY DEBETZ DIET

Be ready to fill in your weight each day on your personal Weight-Loss Record—as you weigh yourself, unclothed, first thing after arising (and attending to your immediate needs, of course) and before eating. Step on the scale and write the number of pounds in the blank space for that day. Then eat according to the food listings for the day.

Use your touch-control stop and support procedures during the day as instructed, in coordination with your eating. At the end of any week, if you still haven't reached your desired weight goal, start with the daily menus again, stopping when the scale shows you the slim-trim number you want.

Must you use the touch-control methods daily? Yes, the "magic touch" is an essential partner of the day-by-day diet provided on the following pages.

REMINDER: As a sparkling daily bonus, you may enjoy with each day's dinner 3 ounces of dry Champagne, or any dry sparkling wine, or any dry white or red wine mixed with salt-free seltzer or club soda, or you may have nonalcoholic sugar-free soda instead. The sparkling bonus drink is optional; you may omit it if you prefer. No other alcoholic drinks are permitted while dieting.

Summary: 10 "Must" Guidelines

1. Use the stop touch-control procedure often.
2. Repeat the support process five to ten times daily.
3. Follow the daily diet listings accurately.
4. Eat moderate portions only. Never heap your plate.
5. Don't drink any high-calorie beverages.
6. Don't use fats in cooking or as additives.
7. Remove all visible fat from servings.
8. Eat plenty of vegetables, as listed for meals.
9. Prevent between-meal snacks with stop action.
10. Never, never overeat. Moderation is the key.

MONDAY

Breakfast

1 small banana or ½ large banana, sliced or other style
½ cup unsugared dry or hot cereal with
4 ounces skim milk
Beverage

Lunch

3 ounces salad of tuna or salmon (water-packed, low-sodium preferably; if tuna is in oil, wash it in a sieve under running water and pat dry with paper towels), plain or with lemon juice, vinegar, low-calorie salad dressing (no more than 16 calories per tablespoon, and no more than 1 tablespoon), or 1 teaspoon of low-calorie imitation mayonnaise. Or use recipes for low-calorie dressings in chapters 5 and 6.
Lettuce, carrots, cherry tomatoes, cucumber, celery
2 low-calorie crackers (melba toast, wafers, crisps, etc.)
Beverage

Dinner

1 cup consommé (preferably low-sodium)
1 moderate slice roast lamb or veal,
Cauliflower or Brussels sprouts, cooked zucchini and onions
Salad of lettuce, radishes, green peppers
½ cup sugar-free applesauce
Beverage

TUESDAY

Breakfast
1 medium orange, sliced or sectioned
½ cup low-fat cottage cheese
1 slice whole-wheat toast
Beverage

Lunch
Hot vegetable plate: spinach, broiled tomato, summer squash, mushrooms, green beans
2 pieces low-calorie melba toast
½ grapefruit
Beverage

Alternate lunch: You may substitute this Tuesday lunch for any other day's with vegetables of your choice of the same calories.

Dinner
6 ounces red snapper, flounder, fillet of sole, or other lean fish
Asparagus spears, broccoli
Salad of watercress, cherry tomatoes, cucumbers
½ cantaloupe or 1 melon slice
Beverage

WEDNESDAY

Breakfast

1 small or ½ large baked apple, no sugar added
1 poached egg on
1 slice whole-wheat toast
Beverage

Lunch

1 moderate slice turkey, all skin and visible fat removed
Salad of lettuce, tomato wedges, shredded cabbage
(as coleslaw, if desired, with seasonings, lemon
juice, vinegar, or low-calorie salad dressing)
Beverage

Dinner

1 cup beef bouillon
4 ounces broiled lean hamburger steak
Broiled tomato, summer squash
Salad of endive, celery, cucumbers
Sugar-free gelatin dessert
Beverage

THURSDAY

Breakfast

3 ounces crushed pineapple in natural juice, no sugar added
½ cup unsugared dry or hot cereal with
4 ounces skim milk
Beverage

Lunch

Fruit salad plate: apple slices, grapefruit segments, sliced half pear or small bunch of grapes, lettuce, topped with 3 ounces low-fat cottage cheese
2 low-calorie flatbread wafers
Beverage

Dinner

1 cup fat-free chicken broth (preferable low-sodium)
6 ounces chicken (skin and all visible fat removed)
Green beans, spinach.
Salad of lettuce, onion, radishes.
½ grapefruit, segmented if preferred
Beverage

FRIDAY

Breakfast
½ grapefruit (use the remaining half from the night before)
½ cup unsugared dry or hot cereal with
4 ounces skim milk
Beverage

Lunch
½ cantaloupe or 1 honeydew wedge
1 cup vegetable soup or clam chowder (no milk or cream), fat-free, low-salt
2 low-calorie bran wafers
Sugar-free gelatin dessert
Beverage

Dinner
1 cup clam broth or consommé (preferably low-sodium)
6 ounces broiled scallops or halibut steak
1 small boiled potato, cooked carrots or small boiled onions
Salad of raw spinach with low-calorie dressing
1 orange, sliced
Beverage

SATURDAY

Breakfast

½ cantaloupe or 6 strawberries
1 egg, boiled or poached or fried or scrambled without fat (use nonstick vegetable spray, if desired)
1 slice whole-wheat toast, with sugar-free fruit spread if desired
Beverage

Lunch

1 cup broth (preferably low-sodium)
3 ounces chicken salad made with a little low-calorie imitation mayonnaise and chopped celery, a few capers, diced green pepper, served on lettuce with carrot and cucumber spears or snow peas
2 pieces melba toast
Beverage

Dinner

4 ounces salt-free tomato juice (may add herbs, spices)
Broiled steak or 1 slice roast beef, lamb, or veal (all visible fat removed)
Asparagus spears, broiled mushrooms
Salad of endive (or lettuce) with green peppers, cherry tomatoes, chives
½ baked apple, no sugar added
Beverage

SUNDAY

Breakfast
½ grapefruit
⅔ cup cooked, unsugared oatmeal or farina or dry cereal
Beverage

Lunch
6 ounces cold fillet of sole or other fish, or shrimp or other shellfish (plain or as salad)
Lettuce or endive, tomato wedges, cold cooked green beans, olives, radishes, red pepper strips
2 low-calorie breadsticks
Beverage

Dinner
4 ounces vegetable juice, low-sodium
6 ounces chicken (broiled, roasted, poached, or barbecued)
Stewed tomatoes, zucchini, combined with eggplant
Salad of mixed greens
Sugar-free gelatin dessert
Beverage

NO-MEAT VARIATION OF THE DEBETZ DIET

If you prefer not to eat any red meat at all, follow the very simple instructions given for the preceding DeBetz Diet. Just make this change: Wherever you see meat listed for a meal, eat chicken, turkey, or fish or shellfish instead. The rest of the meal listing remains the same—vegetables, salad, everything else. You'll probably slim down faster by having lower-calorie poultry or seafood instead of meat. The choice is entirely yours.

SUPPLEMENTAL GUIDELINES

Vital Basic Information

■ **You don't count calories.** As I've emphasized earlier, there's no need to take the time and make the effort to count calories for every meal every day. The total calories in the daily listings, 900 to 1,200, have been counted for you in the makeup of the diet.

For your personal information, if you should wish to check the calorie contents of individual foods and servings—or if you're interested in the protein-fat-carbohydrate composition of a food—you'll find the answers in the comprehensive listings in chapter 12.

It's a good idea, whenever you have the time, to study and learn the calories in the foods you usually eat. Then you can make the best judgments automatically when shopping, eating at home, and eating out. You'll be able to read a menu and add up the approximate number of calories in each item right in your head from memory, as a useful monitor.

■ **Adhere to daily diet listings as printed, but** . . . there will be times when you have to deviate. In such cases, use your good sense and good taste. Shifts are acceptable in instances like this:

When dining out, and choices are limited by the menu listings —or when an item such as a certain vegetable or fruit is out of season and not readily available at the food market where you shop normally, or when a vegetable is too high-priced at one time or another—it's fine to choose another low-calorie vegetable instead. (See the detailed listing of low-calorie vegetables in chapter 12, and make your selections accordingly.)

For example, in a restaurant or friend's home, if spinach, carrots, broccoli, or asparagus is offered instead of the broiled tomato or zucchini on the DeBetz Diet listing that day, certainly you may have the vegetable offered. However, use your good sense—if the asparagus being served is blanketed with hollandaise sauce, refuse it politely. Plain cooked asparagus won't break your diet, but high-calorie melted butter or hollandaise sauce is absolutely forbidden.

If a dinner hostess is serving filet mignon, and the diet dinner listing specifies roast chicken, don't make a fuss. Instead, have the steak without any sauce or gravy, and always a moderate portion, trimming off all visible fat.

Can you have Monday's lamb or veal dinner on Tuesday instead of the fish dinner in the event that you're allergic to fish? Yes. All dinners are about the same number of calories, so are all lunches about the same number of calories. Again, although I recommend following the listings exactly, use good judgment as you observe the general guideline boundaries.

When necessary, it's permissible to eat one dinner instead of another day's listing, or a lunch instead of dinner that day (that's two lunches instead of lunch and dinner); but *never* have two dinners the same day.

Reminder: You can enjoy the delicious Tuesday alternate lunch instead of the lunch listed any other day, as some of my dieters who love vegetables like to do (reread the Tuesday lunch listing). Thus, they have a tasty variety of vegetables at lunch daily—great complex carbohydrates and fiber.

▪ **Use your personal likes** in preparing, serving, and eating the foods specified on the diet plan. For example, for Monday breakfast, you may eat the banana whole or in slices or spears, or even mashed if that's your preference. You may eat the banana separately, or sliced into the cereal. In any of these styles, the banana calories remain the same—and that's what matters on the diet.

▪ **Vitamins, minerals, miscellaneous supplements:** The DeBetz Diet is designed to provide adequate vitamins and minerals for the average dieter. However, you may take a daily vitamin-mineral capsule if you like; that may be beneficial. But don't shovel a lot of extra vitamin and mineral tablets into your body without your physician's approval. Proper use of vitamins and minerals can be good for your health, while overloading can be dangerous. Overdosing with certain elements can be lethal. Follow the advice of your doctor rather than of well-meaning friends whose knowledge is limited or one-sided.

▪ **Don't take drugs or use "reducing devices"** without your physician's recommendation and prescription. Don't take chances with such offerings as "miracle" fish oils, "magical" liquid protein concoctions, "starch blockers," food extenders that swell up in your body, other ballyhooed products such as "body wraps" and "electronic muscle stimulators." Be wary of exhortations by fanatics or extremists. Beware of any inflated advertising claims and promises pushed by commercial interests (their pitches sometimes disguised as public service) who are out for profit with little concern for your personal well-being. Heeding this cautionary advice can help protect your health, even save your life.

■ **Copy the** STOP**lines and** SUPPORT**lines** on a small slip of paper to carry with you as you start my weight-control program. This will serve as a reminder when you go through the stop and support procedures during each day. Very soon the brief lines will become embedded in your consciousness and you won't need the slip to jog your memory.

■ **Remember that you don't have to eat everything on your plate or in the diet listings.** Yes, I've stated this before, but it's so important that it merits repetition. If at any point during a meal you feel full, or prefer to skip a specified serving in the listing for one reason or another, just pass it up—no problem.

■ **Enjoy eating out, but ...** in a restaurant select the foods available that accord with the diet. If dining in someone's home as a guest, skip rich desserts, and rolls and butter or margarine, which would break the diet (as always, use the stop touch action to avoid succumbing to temptation).

Be very specific in your instructions to the waiter or maître d' —for example:

"Broil my fish dry, please." That means no oils, butter, or other fats used in preparation.

"Serve my salad with the dressing on the side, and some lemon wedges and vinegar that I may put on my salad." Of course, "on the side" means that an oily or creamy dressing should not be mixed into the salad ahead of time, nor used at the table if it seems rich and heavy rather than light and fluffy.

"No bread and butter plate for me." Out of sight means out of easy reach, avoids automatic eating, where you hardly realize that you're chewing away.

And always, anytime you're tempted to reach and eat, instead touch and desist.

■ **Keep reviewing the diet guidelines** in this chapter every few days while you are on the diet, repeating the menus each week until you're down to your desired weight. As you proceed to follow the daily menu listings, and are losing pounds and inches steadily, it's also desirable to check your progress with your physician (a phone call is usually sufficient). Helpful as this book can be, it cannot know and keep track of you personally, as your doctor can.

■ **You don't need special recipes** to lose weight on the diet. To help you along if you like to cook, a wide variety of recipes is provided in the next chapter to augment your own cooking talent. You'll note many delicious dishes, and the recipes also serve as guidelines you can follow in preparing your own favorites. They prove beyond doubt that eating on this diet can be gourmet and highly enjoyable as you reduce healthfully and steadily.

■ **"I can't diet for you."** Please note this important example carefully; it makes a significant point. I had just finished instructing a new overweight patient, Faye Lindsay, 27, a television anchorwoman. At the start she had explained, "I've gained so much weight in the past year that my career is suffering. Yet I can't seem to slim down, no matter what I try."

She listened to my instructions attentively, nodding that she understood thoroughly. I handed her my leaflet listing the day-by-day diet. I said, "Here's how you will eat to take off your excess weight, starting tomorrow." She grasped the leaflet and asked emotionally, "Dr. DeBetz, is this *guaranteed* to reduce me and keep me slim at last?"

I said quietly, "Not just holding the leaflet. You have to go on the diet and use the touch-control system faithfully. Only *you* can do that—I can't diet for you."

That was over four years ago. Faye Lindsay slimmed down and has maintained her lovely figure. The same can be true for you, as you follow through day by day according to the detailed, tested, and proved instructions and guidelines in this book.

5

DELICIOUS GUIDELINE DIET RECIPES

Teamed with Touch-Control for Steady Weight Loss

If you like to cook, here's a satisfying assortment of creative lowered-calorie DeBetz Diet recipes as guidance for you. (For vegetarian recipes, see the next chapter.) These delicious, nutritious dishes prove that gourmet food can be prepared to please the palate thoroughly without using any fats or other rich, high-calorie additives. Note that a number of the recipes may be used for a variety of meats, poultry, fish, and shellfish.

Basic recipes for roasting turkey, chicken, beef, or veal are purposely not included, as most individuals have developed their own methods for preparing these roasts. However, do not use any extra oil or fat. Brush with nonfat chicken or beef broth instead, if there is no light layer of natural fat. Where there is a layer of fat, most of it should be removed, leaving only enough to keep food moist. Season to taste with herbs and spices as you like. Baste the roast occasionally with drippings, if there are any, or preferably nonfat broth to keep it from drying out. Be sure to place the roast on a rack in the pan, so fat drips into bottom of pan while cooking.

With all these recipes, the true natural tastes of the good foods themselves come through—that's genuine gourmet food preparation. For finest epicurean servings, delicious innate flavors should never be smothered by rich heavy or fatty sauces, dressings, gravies, or other concealing supplements.

Again, use herbs, spices, and other seasonings lightly to your taste. Be creative with your own variations, always avoiding fats and any other high-calorie additions. Combine textures and colors to appeal to the eye as well as to the tastebuds.

I repeat, these recipes are provided as guidelines if you like to cook. Otherwise, preparation with simple baking, broiling, boiling, and steaming are fine with this diet and for general eating, as many people prefer.

Recipe Listing

CHICKEN, TURKEY

Tender-Baked Whole Chicken

This recipe can be useful as well in preparing fresh turkey parts, which are often available in supermarkets.

3-pound whole chicken (larger chickens tend to have more
    fat)
Garlic powder
Salt, if desired
Paprika
1 large onion, cut into ¼-inch slices
3 ribs celery, cut into 1-inch pieces
½ large apple, cut into ½-inch pieces

1. Have ready a covered casserole just about large enough to hold the chicken. Preheat the oven to 250° F. Wash and dry the chicken, removing any fat you can find. Sprinkle inside and out

with garlic powder, salt if desired, and paprika. Push as much onion, celery, and apple into the chicken cavity as it will hold, and place the chicken, breast down, in the casserole. Surround it with the remaining onion, celery, and apple. Bake, covered, for about 1½ hours.

2. Uncover and bake for 20 minutes longer, until the chicken is very tender and slightly browned. Do not eat the chicken skin. The onion, celery, and apple may be eaten or discarded (certainly discard if any amount of fat has permeated them).

Serves 4 to 6

Chicken Cacciatore

Thick pieces of uncooked turkey breast may be substituted for chicken breasts.

2 medium chicken breasts, cut into 1-inch pieces
¼ cup low-fat chicken broth
1 small green pepper, minced
2 ribs celery, cut across into 1-inch pieces
1 medium onion, chopped
6 large mushrooms, sliced
1 clove garlic, crushed
¼ cup chopped parsley
1-pound can plum tomatoes in tomato purée
3 tablespoons dry white wine
1 teaspoon crushed dried basil or 4 leaves fresh basil,
    chopped
Salt and pepper to taste

1. Spray a large nonstick skillet with vegetable cooking spray. Brown the chicken lightly in a little of the broth, turning until slightly golden. Add the remainder of the broth and the green pepper, celery, onion, mushrooms, garlic, and parsley. Cover, and simmer for 8 minutes, or until the pepper and onion are tender. Add the tomatoes, cut up, wine, and basil.

2. Cook, uncovered, for 10 minutes over medium heat, stirring often with a fork.

Serves 4 or more

Baked Chicken with Mushrooms

3-pound fryer chicken, cut into 8 parts
½ cup nonfat chicken bouillon
2 tablespoons chopped parsley
¼ teaspoon black pepper
¼ teaspoon oregano
¾ teaspoon garlic salt
1 medium onion, very thinly sliced
10 large fresh mushrooms, sliced
3 tablespoons water

1. Remove the skin and all visible fat from the chicken parts. Pat bouillon over the chicken pieces and spread them in a baking pan to just fit without overlapping. Brown quickly under the broiler, about 5 inches from the heat source, turning and brushing with bouillon to prevent drying out. Remove from the broiler. Preheat the oven to 350° F.

2. Sprinkle the chicken with parsley, pepper, oregano, and garlic salt. Spread the onion, mushrooms, and remaining bouillon over the chicken, cover, and bake for 45 minutes to 1 hour, until the onions are cooked through and the chicken is tender. Add more bouillon to the pan while baking to keep the chicken moist if it seems necessary. Sprinkle a little chopped parsley on top when serving, or chopped chives or capers.

Serves 4

Roast Rock Cornish Hen

2 Rock Cornish hens, 1¼ to 1½ pounds each
½ teaspoon salt
3 ribs celery cut into ½-inch pieces
⅛ cup low-fat chicken broth
6 tablespoons no-sugar marmalade

1. Preheat the oven to 350° F. Sprinkle the hens inside and out with salt and pepper. Fill the cavities with celery. Place the

hens on a rack in a small roasting pan, breasts up. Brush with chicken broth and roast, uncovered, for 1 hour, basting with pan drippings and broth at least twice.

2. Mix the remainder of the broth with marmalade and spread the mixture all over the hens. Roast for another 20 to 30 minutes, until crispy brown, basting occasionally with the marmalade mixture and pan drippings. Timing will vary according to the size of the hens.

3. Split them into halves to serve, discarding the celery. Spoon on any leftover sauce. Remove all skin before eating.

Serves 4

Baked Chicken Breasts

2 boned chicken breasts, skin and visible fat removed
½ teaspoon seasoned salt
½ teaspoon mixed herbs
1 cup low-fat chicken bouillon
4 tablespoons dry white wine (do not use cooking wine, as it
    often contains unnecessary salt)
½ teaspoon grated onion or 1 teaspoon chopped fresh or
    frozen chives
½ teaspoon chopped parsley
⅛ teaspoon paprika

1. Preheat the oven to 350° F. Cut the chicken breasts in half lengthwise, rub the pieces all over with seasoned salt and herbs, and place in a single layer in a nonstick baking pan. Mix together the bouillon, wine, onion, and paprika and pour over the chicken. Bake, covered, for 25 minutes (or less, depending on the size of the chicken breasts).

2. Remove the cover, brush the chicken with the juices in the pan, and bake, uncovered, for 10 to 15 minutes, until the chicken is fork-tender. Place the chicken on a warm platter and pour the juice over it to serve.

Serves 4

Chinese Chow Mein

This recipe may be varied by adding pieces of chicken, turkey, cooked beef, lobster, or whole shrimp, if desired, but then omit the rice if you're counting calories and divide into more than 4 servings. Those on a vegetarian diet (see chapter 6) may replace the forbidden ingredients with tofu.

⅓ cup slivered almonds
1 onion, thinly sliced
3 tablespoons nonfat chicken broth or vegetable bouillon
1 cup thinly sliced celery
¼ teaspoon grated fresh ginger (or ⅛ teaspoon powdered ginger)
½ cup bamboo shoots, drained
1 small (5-ounce) can water chestnuts, drained and sliced
1 small white turnip, cut into strips
½ green pepper, cut into ½-inch pieces
1 cup bean sprouts
15 or more snow pea pods
8 to 10 large fresh mushrooms, sliced, or 1 can mushrooms, drained and sliced
1 tablespoon cornstarch
1 cup water
2 tablespoons unsweetened soy sauce
1 cup plain cooked rice
8 to 10 thin slices pimiento

1. Start with the first five ingredients, but you have a choice of any or all of the eight following vegetables. Change quantities to adjust for any vegetables not used.

2. Coat a large skillet (or wok) with vegetable cooking spray. Sprinkle the almonds with a little salt, and sauté until crisp and golden. Remove from the pan and set aside. Sauté the onion in the same pan, with chicken broth and a little more vegetable spray if necessary, stirring until wilted and transparent. Add the celery, ginger, bamboo shoots, water chestnuts, turnip, and green and red peppers; cook for 2 minutes, stirring. Add the remaining vegetables and cook for 2 minutes more.

3. Stir the cornstarch into the water and add with the soy sauce to the vegetables. Lower the heat and simmer for 9 to 10 minutes, stirring, tasting, adding a little more soy sauce if desired. Mix the almonds into the vegetables, and serve over freshly cooked rice. Arrange pimiento strips over the top.

Serves 4

Chicken Spinach Pie

For a delicious vegetarian recipe for those who eat eggs, just omit the chicken or turkey.

2 packages frozen chopped spinach (or chop whole spinach
    leaves in a food processor)
1 teaspoon grated onion or 2 teaspoons chopped chives
Salt to taste
3 eggs
2 slices whole-wheat bread, soaked and squeezed dry
8 ounces low-fat pot cheese
6 tablespoons grated Parmesan or Romano cheese
2 cups of leftover chicken (or turkey) pieces

1. Preheat the oven to 375° F. Thaw the spinach and squeeze out excess liquid. Add the onion and salt. Beat the eggs thoroughly. Separate the wet bread, breaking it up with a fork, and mix all the ingredients together. Coat a 9-inch nonstick pie pan with vegetable cooking spray and press the mixture into it gently.
2. Bake for 40 to 45 minutes, until it is a little firm to the touch and the edges are a little brown. A few capers pressed into the surface add interest.

Serves 4

FISH, SHELLFISH

Broiled Fish Steaks

1½-pound fish steaks (striped bass, cod, halibut, or other
    nonfatty fish), 1 inch to 1½ inches thick, or dressed
    whole sea bass, carp, flounder, red snapper, etc.
¼ teaspoon salt
Pepper
2 teaspoons lemon juice
1 tablespoon minced onion
1 teaspoon (any style, but not dried) mustard
1 tablespoon chopped ripe olives
2 tablespoons dry white wine
¼ teaspoon dried thyme
A little anchovy paste, Worcestershire sauce, pickle relish,
    horseradish (optional)

1. For fish steaks, preheat the broiler. Sprinkle the fish with
salt and pepper. Mix together all the other ingredients and brush
over the fish. Place the fish on a broiler rack (or broil-and-serve
platter) coated with vegetable cooking spray. Broil 2 inches from
the heat for 10 to 15 minutes, depending on thickness, turning
with a spatula and brushing again with the mixture after the first
5 minutes, basting again two or three times more before time is
up. Test with a fork. The fish should flake easily but still be
moist.

2. For whole fish, preheat the broiler. Sprinkle the fish with
salt and pepper, inside and out. Mix together all the other ingredients and brush over and inside fish. (If the fish is split and to
be broiled butterflied, place it on a rack skin side down.) Place
the fish on a broiler rack (or broil-and-serve platter) coated with
vegetable cooking spray. Broil 4 to 6 inches from the heat, depending on the thickness of the fish, for 8 to 10 minutes on the
first side, 10 to 12 minutes on the other side. Baste often while
broiling. Watch the timing, as sizes of fish vary considerably. It
should not be overcooked, but should flake easily with fork and
still be moist.

Serves 4

Basic Marinade Method

Ready-to-cook whole fish has a special flavor when it has been marinated before broiling or grilling. To make a basic marinade, combine in a small bowl 6 tablespoons lemon juice, 6 tablespoons dry white wine, 3 teaspoons chopped fresh herbs or 1½ teaspoons dried mixed herbs (rosemary, mint, chives), salt, and freshly ground pepper. Cut 3 diagonal slashes on each side of the fish, place in a long shallow dish, and brush liberally with marinade (but save some for basting later). Cover and refrigerate for at least 2 hours, and preferably overnight, up to 12 hours. Broil or grill as described above.

Fillets of Fish Florentine

1 pound spinach, cooked and drained
1½ pounds skinned fillets of lean fish
¼ cup white wine
¼ cup nonfat chicken broth
½ teaspoon dried tarragon
¼ teaspoon grated lemon peel, fresh or dried
Salt and pepper to taste
¾ pound cooked shrimp, cut in half lengthwise
½ pound small mushrooms, halved, or 1 can small
    mushroom caps

1. Preheat the oven to 400° F. Coat a large shallow baking dish with vegetable cooking spray and spread the spinach over the bottom. Cover with the fish fillets and sprinkle on a mixture of white wine, chicken broth, tarragon, lemon peel, and salt and pepper. Surround with mushrooms and shrimp.
2. Bake just until heated through, about 10 minutes. Don't overcook!

Serves 4 to 6

"Touch" Bouillabaisse

Lobster, flounder, halibut, or other lean seafood may be used for last four ingredients, not to exceed 1¼ pounds for the entire recipe.

1 cup low-calorie chicken broth
1 cup vegetable broth
1½ cups clam juice
1 cup tomato juice
2 tablespoons lemon juice
1 clove garlic, minced
3 tablespoons minced onion
1 bay leaf
3 tablespoons chopped parsley
⅓ teaspoon thyme
2 tablespoons sherry (optional)
Pinch of saffron, if available
8 ounces cooked scallops
10 ounces cooked red snapper
12 ounces cooked shrimp
10 ounces cooked cod

1. Heat the chicken and vegetable broths together to boiling; lower the heat. Add the juices and all other ingredients except seafood. Simmer for 10 minutes.

2. Meanwhile, cut the fish into 1½- to 2-inch pieces, add with rest of the seafood to the hot liquid, and simmer gently only until very hot, about 4 minutes. Serve in preheated bowls, discarding the bay leaf. Guaranteed to touch the hearts of true gourmets.

Serves 4

Shrimp Scampi

1 teaspoon salt
3 garlic cloves, crushed
1 cup tomato juice
2 tablespoons chopped parsley
1 teaspoon grated onion
¼ teaspoon lemon pepper marinade
¼ teaspoon oregano
Paprika to taste
1½ pounds shelled and deveined medium to jumbo raw
    shrimp, with tails left on if present

1. To make the marinade, mix together all the ingredients except the shrimp. Place the shrimp in the mixture to marinate in the refrigerator for at least 2 hours before cooking.

2. Arrange the shrimp in a shallow broiling pan, pour a little marinade over them, and broil about 3 inches from the heat for 5 minutes on each side—longer if the shrimp are very large, not so long if the shrimp are small. When turning the shrimp over, brush with marinade again, and more often if the shrimp are jumbo size. Do not overcook, or the shrimp will be tough. Sprinkle with a little paprika when serving, if desired. Garnish with lemon slices and watercress.

Serves 4

Poached Salmon with Parsley Sauce

The parsley sauce is delicious with any kind of seafood.

Four 6-ounce salmon steaks
Salt and freshly ground black pepper

Liquid for Poaching (Court Bouillon)

1 lemon, peeled and sliced
1 cup white wine vinegar
1 cup dry white wine
1 bay leaf
1 sprig dill
5 sprigs parsley
1 rib celery, cut up
2 cloves (optional)
2 black peppercorns
1 teaspoon dry mixed herbs
½ teaspoon salt

Parsley Sauce (Delicious with any kind of seafood)

½ cup poaching liquid
½ clove garlic, mashed
2 tablespoons chopped capers
5 tablespoons chopped parsley
1 teaspoon chopped fresh dill or ¼ teaspoon dried
¼ teaspoon salt, or to taste
Celery leaves for garnishing

1. Sprinkle the salmon on both sides with salt and pepper. Put all the ingredients for poaching in a large enough shallow pan so that the fish steaks will not overlap. Bring the liquid to a boil, then simmer. Lay the fish in a single layer in the court bouillon and cover the pan. Gently simmer for about 12 minutes, testing with a fork after 9 minutes, until the fish is no longer transparent and flakes easily.

2. Remove carefully with a spatula to a warm serving platter. Keep warm until the sauce is ready. Strain the poaching liquid

and combine ½ cup of it in a small pan with the other sauce ingredients. Bring to a boil and pour over the fish. Garnish with sprigs of celery leaves (or fresh dill, if you have some).

Serves 4

Lemoned Seafood Salad with Lemon-Mustard Salad Dressing

1 small sweet red pepper
1 medium carrot
2 celery ribs
1 medium red onion, thinly sliced
6 radishes, sliced
1 small cucumber, peeled and sliced
10 to 12 lettuce leaves (or other salad greens)
8 ounces cooked, deveined shrimp (or crabmeat, or lobster, or all three combined)
1 can water-packed solid tuna, drained
10 small pimiento-stuffed green olives, sliced

This lemon-mustard dressing can be used on just about any salads.

4 tablespoons lemon juice
1 clove garlic, crushed
1 teaspoon chopped fresh marjoram or ½ teaspoon dried
½ teaspoon dry mustard
Salt
Pepper

1. Cut the red pepper, carrot, and celery into thin strips. Combine with the onion, radish, and cucumber slices. Arrange the lettuce leaves on 4 salad plates and place mixed vegetables on each. Combine the seafood, lightly flaked tuna, and olive slices, and spoon over the vegetables.
2. Place the dressing ingredients in a small jar, cover, and shake until thoroughly blended. Sprinkle over the salad.

Serves 4

Barbecued Scallop Kabobs

If desired, scallops may be alternated on skewers with cherry tomatoes, parboiled small onions, mushrooms, parboiled green pepper. This sauce is suitable for many kinds of seafood. Try it with halibut steaks, cod steaks, shrimp, etc.

Barbecue Sauce

¼ cup white wine vinegar
½ cup water
¼ cup chili sauce
1 teaspoon grated onion
1 tablespoon Dijon-style mustard
Dash of red pepper
1 tablespoon chopped parsley
1 tablespoon Worcestershire sauce
1 teaspoon (more or less, to taste) "Light Sugar"
1½ pounds large scallops (bay scallops are too small)
Bay leaves
Lemon wedges

1. Stir together all the ingredients for the barbecue sauce except the last, bring to a boil in a small saucepan, then simmer for 15 minutes. Let cool, and add the sweetener.

2. Thread the scallops on skewers, placing a bay leaf between each (or the vegetables listed above). Brush liberally with barbecue sauce. Grill over a low flame, or broil about 4 inches from the heat source, turning often, brushing with sauce. Allow 6 minutes per side for average-size scallops, more for larger, less for smaller. Test with a fork—do not overcook. Serve with barbecue sauce and generous wedges of lemon.

Serves 4

Creamy Shellfish Salad or Dip

1 cup cottage cheese
2 teaspoons lemon juice
1 teaspoon Dijon-style mustard
½ teaspoon salt
⅛ teaspoon lemon pepper marinade
¼ teaspoon Worcestershire sauce
2 cans (about 7 or 8 ounces each) crabmeat
2 cups minced cooked shrimp or 1 can minced clams
2 tablespoons chopped green pepper
Paprika or minced parsley

Process the first six ingredients in a blender or food processor. Add the shellfish and green pepper and process just a little longer. Sprinkle paprika or parsley over the top. May be used as a salad over greens, or for a dip for raw celery, carrot sticks, or slices of cucumber.

Serves 8 (or many more when served as a dip)

BEEF, LAMB, VEAL

Beef, Lamb, or Veal en Brochette

Vegetarians may substitute tofu for meat.

Yogurt Marinade

2 cups yogurt (or buttermilk)
2 cloves garlic, pressed
Salt and pepper to taste
Curry power or ginger to taste (optional)

Pineapple Marinade

¼ cup unsweetened pineapple juice
2 teaspoons soy sauce
2 teaspoons lemon juice
¼ teaspoon fresh or dried lemon rind
1 clove garlic, minced

Ginger Marinade

½ teaspoon turmeric
½ teaspoon powdered ginger or 2 teaspoons grated fresh
    ginger
1 clove garlic, pressed
2 tablespoons lemon juice
Pinch of black pepper

1 pound very lean boneless beef, veal, or lamb
Whole bay leaves or, if desired, cherry tomatoes, parboiled
    red or green pepper pieces, parboiled tiny onions or
    pieces of cut-up regular-size onions, stuffed olives,
    mushrooms, pineapple chunks

1. Mix together the ingredients for one of these marinades in
a bowl just deep enough to accommodate the meat.
2. Cut the meat into 1¼-inch cubes, removing any visible fat.
Place the meat in the bowl and brush the marinade over it,

turning until all parts are covered. Refrigerate for 2 to 3 hours, turning once or twice.

3. Wipe dry and thread onto 4, 5, or 6 skewers, quite close together if you like it rare, with a bay leaf between each cube. If, instead, you choose to alternate vegetables with the meat cubes, the bay leaves may be eliminated. Lay the skewers flat about 3 inches from the source of heat, and grill or broil for about 8 to 10 minutes, brushing with any remaining marinade and turning frequently to brown evenly. If desired, serve on a bed of watercress or shredded lettuce.

Serves 4 to 6

Butterflied Leg of Lamb

Red Wine Marinade

1 cup red wine vinegar
Juice of 1 lemon
1 or 2 cloves garlic, crushed
¾ teaspoon salt
⅛ teaspoon black pepper
1 teaspoon dried tarragon
1 small boned leg of lamb (ask the butcher to butterfly it by
    removing bone and visible fat, pulling off the outer skin,
    and spreading the lamb open like a book)
3 tablespoons chopped parsley

1. Mix all the marinade ingredients. Place the lamb in a shallow baking dish and pour the marinade over it. Turn the lamb to moisten it completely. Cover with foil and refrigerate overnight. In the morning, turn the lamb over again and cover and refrigerate until ready to broil.

2. Preheat the broiler. Place the lamb about 5 inches from the source of heat and broil for 20 minutes on each side, brushing occasionally with marinade to retain moisture. (Test to see whether it is done to your taste a little earlier.) Sprinkle on parsley before serving.

Serves 6 to 8

Veal Balls

Ground beef, lamb, turkey, or chicken may be substituted for veal.

1 pound coarsely ground very lean veal
2 teaspoons lemon juice
2 tablespoons tomato juice or water
1 tablespoon ketchup
¼ teaspoon celery salt
½ teaspoon paprika
¼ teaspoon marjoram
1 egg, lightly beaten
1 cup tomato sauce

1. Coat a medium skillet with vegetable cooking spray. Using a fork, lightly combine all the ingredients except tomato sauce and form the mixture into balls. They can be tiny, or 1 inch or larger.
2. Place in the heated pan, turning until browned all around. Add the tomato sauce, reduce the heat, cover, and simmer for 5 to 10 minutes, according to the size of the balls.

Serves 4

Simple Beef Stew

2 pounds lean round steak or other very lean beef, all visible
    fat removed
2½ cups low-calorie beef broth
4 tablespoons dry red wine
1 large clove garlic, crushed
1 teaspoon salt
Dash of black pepper
4 sprigs parsley, stems tied together
6 ribs celery, thinly sliced
1 pound fresh mushrooms, sliced
½ pound tiny white onions
¾ pound fresh or 1 package frozen green beens

1. Cut the meat into 1½-inch cubes and brown on all sides in a little broth in a heavy saucepan coated with vegetable cooking spray. Pour the remainder of the broth and the wine into the saucepan and add the garlic, salt, pepper, and parsley. Bring to a boil, then cover, lower the heat, and simmer for 1½ hours.

2. Add the celery, mushrooms, onions, and green beans, and simmer for ½ hour longer, or until the meat and onions are tender, adding boiling water if necessary. Discard the parsley before serving.

Serves 6 to 8

Oriental-Style Beef with Vegetables

Very thinly sliced uncooked chicken, turkey, lamb, or veal may be substituted for the steak.

1 pound round steak, all visible fat removed
4 ribs celery, cut into thin diagonal slices
½ pound mushrooms, sliced
½ green bell pepper, thinly sliced
1 small (5-ounce) can sliced water chestnuts
½ cup vegetable bouillon or broth
1 teaspoon grated fresh ginger or ¼ teaspoon powdered ginger
2 tablespoons unsweetened soy sauce
½ pound sliced celery cabbage or fresh spinach leaves (or both, if desired)

1. Freeze the meat briefly so it can be cut easily. Slice very thin diagonally against the grain.

2. Coat a large skillet (or wok) with vegetable cooking spray, heat, add the meat slices, and brown both sides very quickly. Push to one side. Add the celery, mushrooms, and green pepper at the other side of the pan over direct heat and stir and toss for 3 to 4 minutes. Add the rest of the ingredients, mix everything together, cover, and heat for 2 to 3 minutes. Do not overcook.

Serves 4

Continental Stuffed Cabbage

8 large cabbage leaves, blanched (see below)
1 pound ground very lean beef (or lean veal or lamb)
1 egg, beaten
2 tablespoons finely minced onion (or to taste)
3 tablespoons chopped parsley
½ clove garlic, crushed
½ teaspoon thyme
½ teaspoon salt (or more, to taste)
Dash of paprika
Dash of tabasco sauce (optional)
½ cup beef broth
½ cup tomato juice

1. To blanch the cabbage leaves, put them in a large pot of cold water. Bring to a boil, uncovered. Turn the heat down and simmer for 2 minutes. Remove the leaves, drain, and run cold water over them to stop the cooking. Drain again.

2. Preheat the oven to 375° F. With a fork, combine the ground meat with the egg, onion, parsley, garlic, thyme, salt, paprika, and Tabasco sauce. Divide this mixture into 8 parts, placing each part in the center of a cabbage leaf. Roll the ends of the leaves over the stuffing, then fold over the sides and secure with toothpicks.

3. Coat a baking dish with vegetable cooking spray. Arrange the cabbage rolls in the dish, seam side down, in one layer (be sure the dish is not too large—the rolls should just fit) and pour the combined beef broth and tomato juice over them. Cover and bake for 50 to 60 minutes. Pour the remaining sauce over the rolls when serving.

Serves 4

MEAT-STUFFED MUSHROOMS

This same meat mixture may be used for many other recipes. Try stuffed mushrooms: Choose huge "stuffing" mushrooms. Line a muffin pan loosely with aluminum foil, pushing the foil carefully into the depressions; fill each cavity with a mushroom cap. Add chopped mushroom stems to the preceding meat mixture and fill the mushrooms. Sprinkle on lemon juice over stuffed mushrooms and bake for 20 minutes in a 350° F. oven. Allow 3 or 4 mushrooms per person.

Home-Style Cubed Pot Roast

2 pounds round steak, all visible fat removed, cut into large
    cubes
Salt and pepper to taste
½ teaspoon dried thyme
½ cup dry red wine (not cooking wine)
16 small white onions
1 cup sliced fresh mushrooms
3 ribs celery, cut up
1 tablespoon capers
1 bay leaf
1 teaspoon Worcestershire sauce
½ cup water
2 tablespoons chopped parsley

1. Preheat the oven to 350° F. Sprinkle the meat with salt and pepper and thyme. Coat the bottom of a heavy casserole with vegetable cooking spray and a little of the wine, and brown the beef on all sides.

2. Mix the rest of the ingredients except parsley, add to the casserole, cover, and bake for 1½ to 2 hours. Test for tenderness. If the bottom seems to become dry, add a small amount of boiling water and 1 more tablespoon red wine. Sprinkle with parsley before serving.

Serves 6 to 8

Delicious vegetable recipes appear in chapter 6. You'll find them very enjoyable wherever vegetables are listed to cook and serve if you desire.

6

DEBETZ VEGETARIAN DIET
Day-by-Day Listings,
Instructions, Sample Recipes

This is the vegetarian adaptation of the DeBetz Diet. This vegetarian version has proved to be a remarkably effective reducing and weight-control program for vegetarians I have treated in my medical practice over the past 16 years. Aside from the elimination of poultry, fish, shellfish, and meats . . . follow all the touch-control and other instructions and recommendations throughout this book.

Many vegetarians have a sweet tooth, and add to their very healthful diets quantities of rich desserts, honey, candies, and chocolates, as well as thickly buttered breads and rolls and pastries. Accordingly, many vegetarians are considerably overweight. My diet is nutritious, satisfying, and filling, while bypassing such high-calorie foods. You will find the natural tastes of simply prepared vegetables and dairy products delicious.

Note that protein foods are included daily. Protein is an essential nutrient, which your body needs for proper functioning.

There are many variations among types of vegetarians. Some eat eggs; others add poultry and fish and still consider themselves vegetarians. My plan is designed for those who do not eat these foods, but if you want them, you may alter the guideline recipes, adding ingredients to suit yourself. But watch your calories; although you need not count calories, you must avoid any added fattening foods while on this effective reducing diet.

When preparing mixed vegetable recipes, avoid those that are starchy or fatty, such as avocados, peas (may have in small quantities), sweet potatoes, lima beans, other dry beans, or corn, except where specifically named in the vegetarian diet menus. Avoid dried fruits, also; they are extremely high in calories.

As a substitute for the lunch or dinner on these menus, whenever you like you may have clear broth, mixed vegetables and tofu, hot or cold, with a baked potato or ½ cup plain white or brown rice or cooked soybeans.

Do try to emphasize dark green leafy vegetables.

Unsweetened soy sauce or tamari (a salty soy derivative available in some stores) may be used in moderation for flavoring, as well as herbs and spices of your choice, garlic, parsley, or grated onion.

Cottage cheese, processed with skim milk in a blender, makes a substitute for sour cream.

For a snack, heat tomato juice or nonfat vegetable or onion bouillon, adding lemon juice and herbs to taste, or grate into it a little tasty Romano or Parmesan cheese. Sprinkle chopped chives, sliced scallions, shaved mushrooms, chopped parsley, or toasted sesame seeds on top.

Tofu, a soybean product made from soybean milk, is low-sodium, high in protein, low in calories, and often used as a substitute for meat and cheese. Mashed, it can sometimes serve as a replacement for cottage cheese or ricotta cheese in cooking and dressings. Cubed, it can be stir-fried in place of meat or tossed in salads, or seasoned and broiled. Buy fresh tofu, if available. A good tip is to freeze it, then slice it and sauté in sugar-free soy sauce in a nonstick pan.

Toasted sesame seeds add texture and flavor when sprinkled over vegetables or a baked potato. When steaming vegetables, don't ignore cauliflower, broccoli, Brussels sprouts, cabbage, parsnips, leeks, cabbage, fennel, turnips, kale, kohlrabi, artichoke hearts, Chinese cabbage, okra, sweet red peppers, and many more familiar dark green vegetables. Mixtures of colors and textures can make foods even more delicious.

Salads, of course, are an important part of a vegetarian diet. In addition to the two dressing recipes at the end of this chapter, you may use any bottled or homemade low-calorie dressing (no more than 16 calories per tablespoon). Also, refer to the lemon mustard dressing on page 65.

If you eat eggs, see the Spinach Pie on page 59. You'll find other recipes in chapter 5 that may be varied to suit your diet requirements, such as Beef, Lamb, Veal en Brochette, in which you will want to substitute tofu for the meat. You will find Chow Mein in that chapter, also; just leave out the nonvegetable ingredients and replace with tofu, if you like.

Beverage listing at meals (and any time you want a beverage between meals) includes hot or iced coffee, tea (preferably decaffeinated), no-calorie carbonated sodas in your choice of flavors, and sugar-free club soda, seltzer, naturally carbonated water, and, of course, plain water—as many glassfuls as you can drink comfortably per day.

REMINDER: As a sparkling daily bonus, you may enjoy with each day's dinner 3 ounces of dry Champagne, or any dry sparkling wine, or any dry white or red wine with salt-free seltzer or club soda, or you may have nonalcoholic sugar-free soda instead. The sparkling bonus drink is optional; you may omit it if you prefer. No other alcoholic drinks are permitted while dieting.

DAILY VEGETARIAN DIET MENUS

MONDAY

Breakfast

1 small banana or ½ large banana, sliced or other style
½ cup unsugared dry or hot cereal with
4 ounces skim milk
(See recipe for Microwave Hot Cereal in this chapter, if you would like to follow it)
Beverage

Lunch

Marinated mixed vegetable salad: raw vegetables such as mushrooms, zucchini, snow peas, green beans, bean sprouts, with low-calorie salad dressing, tossed with
1 ounce feta cheese, broken and sprinkled over salad
(See recipe for Flavor-full Cold Vegetables in this chapter, if you would like to follow it)
½ cantaloupe, cubed if desired
Beverage

Dinner

1 cup clear vegetable broth with floating shaved mushrooms and toasted sesame seeds
Cooked mixed vegetables with lemon juice
Baked rice-stuffed green bell pepper
(See recipe for Rice-Stuffed Tomato or Green Pepper in this chapter, if you would like to follow it)
2 rye wafers
Sugar-free fruit cocktail
Beverage

TUESDAY

Breakfast
1 orange, sliced or sectioned
1 slice whole-wheat toast with apple butter
Beverage

Lunch
1 cup mixed vegetable juice
Sliced mixed fruit with low-fat cottage cheese and chopped nuts, on Romaine or Bibb lettuce (or other greens)
(See recipe for Beautiful Fruit in this chapter, if you would like to follow it)
2 slices melba toast
Beverage

Dinner
1 cup onion soup topped with grated cheese and whole-wheat croutons
1 medium baked potato with yogurt and chives
Mixed steamed vegetables
½ grapefruit
Beverage

WEDNESDAY

Breakfast
1 small or ½ large baked apple, no sugar added
½ cup unsugared dry or hot cereal with
4 ounces skim milk
Beverage

Lunch
½ cup tomato juice
Yellow squash prepared with apple and nutmeg
(See recipe for Nutmeg Squash in this chapter, if
you would like to follow it)
Chilled asparagus sprinkled with lemon juice
Mixed green salad with ½ ounce diced part-skim
cheese, low-calorie dressing, and 3 medium ripe
olives
Beverage

Dinner
1 cup clear vegetarian soup
½ eggplant with tomato sauce, grated Parmesan
cheese, and part-skim mozzarella cheese
(See recipe for Eggplant Parmesan in this chapter,
if you would like to follow it)
Moderate size salad of lettuce, raw spinach, cucumbers, sliced carrots, radishes, with low-calorie
dressing
½ cup unsweetened applesauce mixed with 2
tablespoons chopped pecans
Beverage

THURSDAY

Breakfast

½ cup crushed pineapple, no sugar added
2 slices melba toast
1 teaspoon low-calorie fruit preserves or jelly
½ cup plain low-fat yogurt or low-fat pot cheese
Beverage

Lunch

1 cup onion broth or miso soup
Mixed marinated cold vegetables with tofu
(See recipe for Flavor-full Cold Vegetables in this chapter, if you would like to follow it)
2 rye wafers
1 ounce cheese, preferably part-skim, or ½ cup low-fat pot or cottage cheese, or 1 tablespoon peanut butter
Beverage

Dinner

1 cup vegetable juice with a squeeze of lemon
Ratatouille: eggplant, onion, pepper, zucchini, tomato combination
(See recipe for Ratatouille in this chapter, if you would like to follow it)
½ cup cooked soybeans
½ cantaloupe or 1 small wedge of other melon
Beverage

FRIDAY

Breakfast
½ grapefruit
½ cup unsugared dry or hot cereal with
4 ounces skim milk
Beverage

Lunch
1 cup low-calorie cranberry juice
Chilled cauliflower with curried sauce
(See recipe for Chilled Curried Cauliflower in this
chapter, if you would like to follow it)
Broiled tomato sprinkled with Parmesan cheese
(See recipe for Broiled Tomato in this chapter, if
you would like to follow it)
1 medium baked potato topped with ⅓ cup plain
yogurt and toasted sesame (or other) seeds
Beverage

Dinner
1 cup clear vegetable soup with carrot splinters,
very thin uncooked zucchini slices, and grated
cheese
Chow mein
(See recipe for Chow Mein in chapter 5, if you
would like to follow it)
2 low-calorie bread sticks
½ cantaloupe
Beverage

SATURDAY

Breakfast

1 orange, sliced or sectioned
1 slice whole-wheat (or other whole-grain) bread
1 tablespoon peanut butter
Beverage

Lunch

1 cup vegetable juice
Green pepper stuffed with rice
(See recipe for Rice-Stuffed Tomato or Green Pepper in this chapter, if you would like to follow it)
Moderate-size salad of shredded cabbage, watercress, other salad greens, cold cooked vegetables, sliced olives, with lemon juice and herbs
2 rye wafers with sugar-free preserves
Beverage

Dinner

Gazpacho
(See recipe for Gazpacho in this chapter, if you would like to follow it)
Asparagus broiled with 1 ounce part-skim cheese over it
½ cup cooked soybeans
Marinated mushrooms
(See recipe for Mushrooms Prepared in Marinade in this chapter, if you would like to follow it)
Beverage

SUNDAY

Breakfast
Fresh fruit cup
½ cup unsugared dry or hot cereal with
4 ounces skim milk
Beverage

Lunch
1 cup light vegetable soup
Salad of ⅓ cup cold cooked soybeans, ½ cup cubed tofu, greens, tomato wedges, low-calorie dressing
½ cup sugar-free applesauce with 2 tablespoons chopped walnuts
Beverage

Dinner
1 medium baked potato with yogurt and chives or toasted sesame seeds
Baked eggplant and zucchini with ½ ounce part-skim mozzarella cheese
Moderate-size salad of radishes, cucumbers, grated carrot, greens, with mustard or vinaigrette dressing (See last two recipes in this chapter and lemon-mustard dressing for Lemoned Seafood Salad in chapter 5, if you would like to use one of them)
1 medium pear poached in wine (See recipe for Wine-Poached Pears in this chapter, if you would like to use it)
Beverage

VEGETARIAN RECIPES

Chilled Curried Cauliflower

Asparagus or broccoli may be substituted for cauliflower.

1 large head of cauliflower
2 carrots, cut lengthwise into strips
1 cucumber, sliced diagonally
1 cup plain low-fat yogurt
1 tablespoon Dijon-style mustard
1 teaspoon seasoned salt
Black pepper
½ teaspoon curry powder (or to taste)

1. Steam the whole cauliflower until tender. Place on a platter in refrigerator to chill.
2. When chilled, arrange the carrot strips and cucumber slices around it. Blend the rest of the ingredients into a sauce, and spoon over the vegetables to serve.

Serves 4

Broiled Tomato

2 large tomatoes, cut across into halves
2 teaspoons lemon juice
1 teaspoon fresh or frozen chives
½ teaspoon garlic salt (or less, to taste)
2 teaspoons grated Parmesan cheese

Preheat the broiler. Place the tomato halves in a shallow oven-proof baking pan, about 5 inches from the heat source. Sprinkle with lemon juice, chives, garlic salt, and Parmesan cheese. Broil until very hot and slightly softened.

Serves 4

Nutmeg Squash

1 package frozen cooked yellow squash
¼ teaspoon salt
1 apple, peeled, cored, and cut into ¼-inch pieces
3 tablespoons water
4 tablespoons chopped walnuts or pecans
Sprinkle of nutmeg

1. Preheat the oven to 350° F. Thaw and heat the squash, and add salt. Cook the apple pieces in water for a few minutes until tender; drain if necessary.
2. Combine the apple with the squash and place in an oven-proof dish. Sprinkle on walnuts and nutmeg and bake for 5 to 8 minutes, until very hot.

Serves 3 or 4

Light Vegetable Soup

This may be varied by adding tofu cubes, or by substituting 1 cup tomato juice for 1 cup vegetable broth, or both.

5 cups nonfat vegetable broth or bouillon
2 slices fresh ginger
3 cups cut-up or sliced raw vegetables (green beans, carrots,
    zucchini, asparagus, white turnip, shredded cabbage,
    etc., alone or in combination)
2 scallions, sliced very thin
2 sprigs parsley or watercress

Bring the broth and ginger to a boil and simmer for 2 minutes. Add the vegetables, bring to a boil again, and simmer for 5 minutes longer. Remove ginger, and serve the soup in 4 deep bowls, scattering sliced scallions and parsley on each serving.

Serves 4 or more

Ratatouille

2 medium green peppers, sliced thin
2 medium onions, sliced thin
1 large clove garlic, mashed
3 tablespoons nonfat vegetable broth or bouillon, or
    vegetable juice or tomato juice
1 medium eggplant, cut into ¾-inch dice
3 small or 2 medium zucchini, cut into ¼-inch slices
6 medium or 4 large fresh tomatoes, peeled and chopped
⅓ cup chopped parsley
1 to 2 teaspoons salt, or to taste
Freshly ground black pepper to taste
10 small pimiento-stuffed green olives, sliced

1. Lightly sauté the green peppers, onions, and garlic in broth
in a very large nonstick pan until the onions are transparent and
limp. Add the garlic, eggplant, zucchini, and tomatoes, cover,
and simmer for about 30 minutes (test the vegetables with a fork
for desired tenderness).

2. Add the parsley and simmer gently, stirring occasionally,
for 8 to 10 minutes more. If mixture seems too thin, simmer a
little longer. Stir in the olives. Serve hot or cold.

Serves 4 to 8

Beautiful Fruit

1 cup sliced mixed fruit and/or berries (if canned, be certain
    the syrup is no-sugar-added)
Romaine or Bibb lettuce or any salad greens you choose
½ cup low-fat cottage or pot cheese
¼ cup plain low-fat yogurt
2 tablespoons chopped walnuts or pecans

Serve the fruit over the greens, topped with cheese, then yogurt, then nuts. Garnish with mint leaves, if you like.

Serves 1

Rice-Stuffed Tomato (or Green Pepper)

4 large tomatoes
1 cup cooked rice
2 ounces shredded Cheddar or American cheese, part-skim if
    available
2 tablespoons chopped parsley
Salt and black pepper

1. Preheat the oven to 350° F. Slice about ¼ inch from the
tops of the tomatoes. Scrape out some of the tomato pulp to
make room for the stuffing, leaving about ½ inch of tomato
shell.
2. Mix the rest of the ingredients, saving a little cheese for
topping, and spoon the mixture into the tomato shells. Sprinkle
the rest of the cheese on top. Bake until the tomatoes are tender,
for about 20 minutes, depending on size.

Serves 4

Gazpacho

2 large soft tomatoes, peeled
1 clove garlic, halved
1 medium red onion, quartered
1 cucumber, peeled and quartered
3 tablespoons chopped parsley
2 tablespoons chopped basil or 2 teaspoons dried
2 tablespoons chopped chives
3½ cups tomato juice
2 tablespoons lemon or lime juice
Salt, pepper, paprika

Process all the vegetables together in a food processor. Add
the rest of the ingredients, mix well, and serve well chilled.

Serves 4

Flavor-full Cold Vegetables

You may omit any of the suggested ingredients and make your own combination. Include a small amount of cooked soybeans, if you wish.

2 small zucchini, sliced on the diagonal, parboiled, and
    chilled
16 snow peas, trimmed, parboiled, and chilled
1 cup young green beans, cut up, parboiled, and chilled
1 cup sliced mushrooms
½ sweet red pepper, sliced or in small chunks
½ cup bean sprouts
1 small can bamboo shoots, drained
8 cooked artichoke heart halves, prepared without oil
8 small broccoli florets
8 small cauliflower florets
Cubed tofu, all you want
Marinade

Marinade

2 cups nonfat vegetable stock or bouillon
4 tablespoons dry white wine
6 tablespoons lemon juice
1 large clove garlic, mashed
½ cup chopped parsley
½ teaspoon thyme
1 teaspoon Worcestershire sauce
1 teaspoon salt
Black pepper to taste

1. Cook the zucchini, snow peas, and green beans in boiling water for 2 minutes. Drain immediately and chill.
2. Bring all the marinade ingredients to a boil, then simmer for 30 minutes.
3. Arrange the vegetables on a platter and pour on enough marinade to coat them all. Cover with foil and refrigerate for at least a few hours before serving. Any remaining marinade will

keep in refrigerator for a few days. When serving, you may wish to top with some alfalfa sprouts or thin sweet onion slices.

Serves 4

MUSHROOMS PREPARED IN MARINADE
You might want to put some tiny mushrooms in a jar, cover with leftover marinade, and refrigerate for later use.

Eggplant Parmesan

1 medium eggplant, cut across into ¼-inch slices
12 ounces crushed tomatoes in purée (or use tomato sauce)
2 teaspoons chopped parsley
1 teaspoon grated onion (or 2 teaspoons chopped chives)
5 tablespoons grated Parmesan cheese
½ clove garlic, crushed
1 teaspoon dried oregano
½ teaspoon salt
Black pepper to taste
3 ounces part-skim mozzarella cheese, sliced very thin

1. Simmer the eggplant slices in slightly salted boiling water for 3 minutes. Drain and pat dry with paper towels. Coat a large nonstick skillet with vegetable cooking spray and brown the eggplant on both sides. Repeat until all eggplant is browned. (You may prefer to use two skillets at once, to save time.)
2. Preheat the oven to 375° F. Combine the tomatoes, parsley, onion, grated cheese (reserving a little for topping), garlic, oregano, salt, and pepper. Pour a little of this sauce into the bottom of a shallow baking pan, then add a layer of eggplant, then mozzarella cheese, then sauce, etc., alternating until the eggplant is used up. The top layer should be sauce. Sprinkle with a little grated Parmesan cheese. Bake for 35 minutes, or until hot and bubbly.

Serves 3 or 4

Microwave Hot Cereal

For a filling breakfast.

Water, double the amount indicated on the packet
1 packet instant farina or oatmeal
4 ounces skim milk

In a deep bowl, bring water to a boil in a microwave oven. Remove from the oven and sprinkle in the instant cereal, mixing well. Add the milk, stir, replace in the microwave oven, and bring to a boil again. If you prefer it thicker, boil a little longer. Note that it will thicken more after you remove it from the oven. With experience, you will learn just how much water you wish to add. The more you use, the more filling the cereal will be.

Serves 1

Wine-Poached Pears

4 medium Bosc pears, peeled and cut into halves
6 tablespoons lemon juice
1½ cups water
1 cup dry red wine (not cooking wine, as it usually contains
    other ingredients)
4 whole cloves
1 cinnamon stick, broken in half
1 teaspoon artificial sweetener (Aspartame, NutraSweet), if
    desired

1. Rub the pear halves with lemon juice to prevent surface browning. Put the water, wine, cloves, and cinnamon in a saucepan and bring to a boil. Place pears in this liquid, cover, and poach for 8 to 9 minutes, more or less according to the size of the pears. Test with a fork; they should not be too soft.

2. Let cool in the sauce, and mix 1 teaspoon sugar substitute into the sauce before serving. Pour a few tablespoons of sauce over each portion of 2 pear halves.

Serves 4

Mustard Dressing for Salads

¼ cup Dijon-style mustard
¼ cup white wine vinegar
⅓ cup low-fat yogurt
1¼ cups chopped chives
¼ cup chopped parsley
¼ teaspoon garlic salt
Dash of black pepper
Artificial sweetener to taste (optional)

Shake the ingredients together in a small covered jar. Use on salads or chilled vegetables. Keep refrigerated.

Makes 2 + cups

Vinaigrette Salad Dressing

1 cup red wine vinegar
4 teaspoons chopped fresh parsley or 1 teaspoon dried
4 teaspoons grated onion, or to taste
1 large clove garlic, crushed
2 tablespoons capers
4 teaspoons finely chopped pimiento
2 tablespoons cold water
Salt, black pepper, paprika to taste

Place all the ingredients in a small jar, cover tightly, and shake well each time the dressing is used. It will keep for some time in refrigerator.

Makes 1 + cups

7

SHIFTING EMPHASIS TO BODY FROM FOOD

Erase "Fat-Eating" Habits from Now On

It is extremely important that you carefully read every word of this chapter (as well as all the others). What you will learn and put into practice can be of special benefit in promoting not only your steady weight loss and control, but also better health life-long. The process of shifting your peak attention to your body, now and in the future—instead of on food, as in the past—can assure that you'll achieve and maintain your desired body weight at any age.

EMPHASIZE "BODY" IN THE STOPLINES

By this time, repeating the three STOPlines, along with the comforting touch on your face, has become second nature to you. Now, privately, repeat the STOPlines aloud to yourself as an object lesson. Emphasize the word body each time, this way:

For my body, overeating is an insult and a poison.
I need my body to live.
I owe my body this respect and protection.

Did you notice how the emphasis on the one word resulted in peak concentration on *body* in your consciousness? From this time forward, I want you to emphasize the word *body* in your thinking as you use the STOPlines silently to obliterate any food temptation that may arise. Repeat it wherever and whenever the idea of *food* lures you to break your diet.

In creating the DeBetz Diet system, and perfecting it through testing and treatment over the years, I found it essential to stress *body* as an integral part of the three STOPlines. As you keep doing this, you will be changing your past destructive attitude about food and eating. Your focus on your body will become far more significant, and then dominant.

The all-important, crucial difference working for you here is that instead of someone telling you, or you telling yourself, to get your mind off food, now you'll possess and use the how-to, the actual way, the tool that shifts your mind away from food. The emphasis will shift to the slimmed, attractive body image you seek. With your new tools at hand, at last you'll slim down and stay trim as you could not up to now . . . as so many others have done with these methods.

DOES YOUR BODY DESERVE THIS RESPECT AND ATTENTION?

I'd like you now to repeat aloud, or to yourself, the third STOPline: "I owe my *body* this respect and protection." Think of the meaning behind that statement, not just the words themselves. The last thing I'll ever do is lecture to you—I'm sure you've had too much of that in your life. Nor do I aim to frighten you. So bear with me as I stress a few basic truths about the medical linkage between overweight and bodily health.

While appearance is generally the outstanding reason why many individuals want to lose weight (whether they acknowledge it or not), I'm sure that your health is of vital concern to you. Seeking maximum good health is certainly potent in helping you shift your emphasis to achieving and maintaining a healthy, trim body.

There's no dodging established fact, as doctors attest, that the incidence of a number of common diseases and afflictions is significantly higher among overweight persons compared with their normal-weight peer group. It's not difficult to realize that overweight can be associated with damage to weight-bearing joints such as knees, hips, and lower back. Obviously, overload a branch and it breaks.

It's not so obvious to many that overweight, even as little as 10 excess pounds, can be associated with some chronic diseases, afflictions that may eventually threaten life if untreated. Nevertheless, although I could fill another volume with detailed explanations about how dangerous it could be to your health to remain overweight, let's examine just a few primary hazards to your vibrant health and long life. Among the more prevalent threats are:

Hypertension (High Blood Pressure)

Nobody can argue against the findings from a screening of more than a million individuals, which revealed this significant fact: A far larger percentage of those who were overweight recorded an elevation in blood pressure, many in the high danger zone, compared with normal-weight people. But here's encouragement for you: A considerable number of overweight men and women with high blood pressure can reduce the pressure just by losing weight.

Diabetes

Note this shocking fact: In addition to family-related and inherited factors that play a role, it has been found that some 80 percent of newly diagnosed diabetics are overweight. Now the good news: Diabetes that appears in adult life can often be satisfactorily controlled by diet alone.

Heart Disease

Life insurance data has shown that deaths linked to cardiovascular and kidney disease were about 50 percent more among overweight people than expected on the basis of normal mortality. Here again, happily, statistical comparisons reveal that overweight persons who then reduced to normal weight had mortality rates comparable to those of the normal population.

The relationship between overweight and many more afflictions and diseases than the three I've mentioned here is factual and frightening, but I prefer not to alarm you excessively. I do want to stress that when you reduce to your normal weight, you give yourself a better chance to live longer, more healthily, more happily, and, last but not least, more attractively.

A bright science researcher, Jennifer Gertner, 29, said, "Statistics tied overweight to so many sicknesses that I knew I had to dump at least 20 pounds to enjoy a vigorous long life. So every time I did my touch-control and STOPlines, I'd finish by telling myself, 'Good-bye, sickness—hello, healthy body!' Now that I'm slim, I've promised myself that I'll never add unhealthy pounds again."

ACCENT ON THE POSITIVE

You've noticed that throughout this book I've accented the positive aspects of weight control rather than seeking to make you feel deprived or guilty. I tell you exactly what you can *do* to slim down and make things better. My two-way touch-control system is designed to improve your life-style, to work for you as it has worked for others.

My emphasis isn't on scolding: "*Don't* eat fatty foods. *Don't* eat rich chocolate and ice cream. *Don't* do this, *don't* do that." My thrust is on your developing positive thoughts and attitudes, thus shifting your peak concentration to what you're for rather than focusing on what you're against. You are for the health and appearance of your body, right?

Good. Realize enthusiastically that you are embarked on a new learning experience. You will learn most effectively how to slim down permanently this time through the positive do's you'll acquire rather than pressure upon don'ts. Think of your touch-control and DeBetz Diet combination in the same way— all positives, banishing negatives.

One of your greatest aids is knowing that you are learning

new ideas, new ways of doing things, tested and proved new methods that will work for you. Realizing that "knowledge is power" increases your personal power to control your weight. You add to your knowledge and power by acquiring certain basic truths about your body as it relates to weight.

You'll learn that in addition to healthful eating, your body needs to be active. With this tested and proved touch-plus-diet system, it is possible at last for you to succeed in losing weight. Your personal positive attitude, setting aside any negative aspects, will lead to success: improved appearance and better health.

Of course, different individuals have different weight problems. There's no end to the theories of why people are overweight—the "fat cell" hypothesis, the thesis that each has a "setpoint," the concepts of heredity, environment, childhood feeding patterns, on and on. But the fact is that if you are motivated, and accept that you must make a special effort, then you can have high hopes that you will finally reach your goal of lowered body weight.

Whatever else, realized that *this is your body, and that as you take charge and control, you can have a slim body.* The more important it is to you to be slim, the more steadfastly you'll follow my advice and instructions. So I urge that, rather than feeling angry or resentful of your overweight body, you focus on changing it; start working on your body transformation. How? Protect your body from the damage due to overeating, and do it, starting now, in the following specific ways that work.

SHIFTING YOUR FOCUS TO
YOUR BODY BEAUTIFUL

Telling you to "think thin," as others have undoubtedly told you in the past, simply doesn't function in any practical way to help you reduce. It's like a swimming instructor ordering, "swim," and then pushing you into the water. Just thinking "swim" results in drowning. Just thinking "thin" usually submerges the hapless overweight in more excess pounds. You've probably learned that the hard way.

To help you really shift your concentration away from food, and directly and effectively to slimming your body, I developed two extra easy-to-use fortifying sequences that have worked splendidly for my patients. Do these each once daily at a time of your choice, aside from your regular stop and support procedures. They'll help you keep focused and successful in taking off your excess weight steadily, and take only a few minutes to complete.

1. Mirror Body Image

Standing erect, preferably nude but wearing clothes if that's more convenient, look at yourself critically in a full-length mirror. Examine your appearance slowly; take inventory of your face (too rounded?), chin (double chin? sagging jowls?), shoulders and arms (bulky?), breasts (overly full or pendulous?), abdomen, hips, buttocks (bulging?), legs (thickened?).

Be honest with yourself as you take stock of the negatives, particularly in this examination. Assure yourself that the time of denial is over. No more blocking out reality. No more hiding under loose gowns or cleverly deceptive tailoring.

Now, after a moment of brutally frank self-appraisal, make a shift to a mental snapshot of how much more attractive you'll look to yourself and others after you take off disfiguring excess pounds and inches. Realize what a pleasure it will be then to see your trim, firm body. That quick interval of self-asssessment will reinforce your commitment to achieve your own "body beautiful," and keep it lovely and limber.

Repeating this mirror examination each day or evening will be a super-boost. You'll find each brief sequence refreshing and sustaining.

2. TV-Screen Body Transformation

You'll deeply enjoy this short voyage of the imagination. Seat yourself in a comfortable chair. Relax your body thoroughly . . . ahhhh. Close your eyes. Take a slow, deep breath, then exhale. Loosen up, feel at ease . . . mmmm.

Now that you have cleared away worries and tensions from your body and mind, do this: Eyes still closed, imagine that you are looking at a large TV screen in your mind (or a movie screen, or even a blank wall). On the imaginary screen, project the image of your naked body today—10 or 20 or more pounds overweight. Now, as you are viewing your body in your mind's eye on the screen, see your body slimming down . . . gradually, steadily, surely . . .

Keep looking at the thrilling transformation that is taking place. Scan your naked body slowly as you view the delightful changes . . . face and chin and other areas firmed . . . arms, legs, torso slimmed beautifully all over. Delight in your newly trimmed body, which will be admired by yourself and others . . .

In the past, you've probably had the same unsettling experience as a patient I saw recently, Deborah Bergen, 39, personnel manager in a small firm. "I've gained 30 pounds in the past three years after a long love affair broke off suddenly," she explained. "I was so unhappy that I concentrated on eating, regardless of my appearance. Now I'm waking as if from a dream. Looking in the mirror at those awful bulges, I feel like a stranger in my own body. Please help me find myself slim and attractive again."

Realize that we all become familiar with our bodies, in a positive or negative way. You take your body for granted until you become aware of the ugly or beautiful transformation. After Ms. Bergen had taken off the 30 disfiguring pounds, she told me, "It's so strange—when I walk down the street now and catch my reflection in the window glass, I have to take a second look to recognize that it's me. I guess it'll take a little time to get used to my new slim body again—but I love it!"

Yes, you do have to get used to your newly slimmed body, and other feelings that go with it. Be proud—look in the mirror, pay attention to your body. Look at your it—touch, feel. The more comfortable you are with your body, and the more important your bodily well-being is to you, the more certain it is that you'll stay trim all your life.

The TV-screen body shape-up is especially essential if you overeat through nervousness, worry, dejection, all types of negative pressure. Instead of reaching for food in the hope that it will calm you down, take a few minutes for the relaxing, comforting TV-screen transformation. Food is not a tranquilizer. It won't quiet your nerves—but sitting back, closing your eyes, breathing deeply, and scanning the delightful body transformation on your mental screen will soothe you wonderfully.

Do it now if you can take a moment—and at least once each day or evening. You'll be joining your mind and body in a positive, slimming-trimming way, rather than in a negative abusive way by overfeeding it. Using these two refreshing, supportive shape-ups, along with the other touch-control procedures and the nutritious DeBetz Diet, will help change your focus lifelong to body from food. Thus, you can achieve your goal of transforming your body, not into unrealistic perfection, but into the healthiest, most beautiful it can be.

Take it from me, after years of gratifying experience with all types of women and men—*the system works as you work with it.*

8

ESSENTIAL MEDICAL-
PSYCHOLOGICAL
PLUSES
Vital Physical-Emotional Support

You'll find the recommendations in this chapter of singular benefit, since *you've never found this tested and proved medical-psychological counsel in any diet book before.* Coordinating your new enlightenment with the touch-control techniques and the DeBetz Diet, you'll attain your most desired weight control goals.

In the past, diets have listed *what* to eat. Now you'll use directions of prime importance on *how* to eat and how to *think* about eating. When you absorb all this needed information, you'll be able to apply most efficiently the easy-to-use instructions to stay trim for the rest of your life. (You'll be benefiting from what professionals call "cognitive restructuring.")

Now, please stop blaming yourself for past failures in reducing and maintaining your desired weight. You were never told the essentials of how your senses and your emotional makeup, as well as your physical system, are involved in eating and overeating. Combining such emotional and physical eating know-how can work for you in a way you never knew was possible.

Be optimistic, based on your newly acquired knowledge. Your optimism will be a stimulant to success. You'll know how to perceive, use, and control your senses effectively in practical ways that influence your eating and weight. Read carefully; use this good-sense information about the senses along with the diet and touch-control procedures. You'll attain the trim, healthier, more beautiful body you seek.

THE SENSE OF TOUCH

By now, practicing the stop and support sequences, as instructed, you have already become more conscious of and improved your sense of touch, far beyond the usual. You have felt the warmth and lift of the intimate contact of your fingertips on your face. You have experienced how that signal turns on peak concentration and links your emotional and physical powers for maximum self-control.

As you know, the "magic touch" stops you from eating food that's too rich and from overeating. No matter how skeptical you might once have been, experiencing the touch has made you a believer. Increasingly, being aware of the potency in your sense of touch, and knowing how to use it, is vital in sustaining your diet to take off the excess pounds.

The normal human is born with a keen sense of touch. In the infant, touch-feel is one of the predominant senses to be developed. We use touch often without realizing it fully. Think of your last trip to the supermarket—didn't you reach out and touch the tomatoes, melons, other foods, to get the feel of their quality?

Apply this awareness to your eating beneficially on the diet and after. Obviously, we don't touch all our food with our fingers, but the fork and knife are an extension of our fingers, in effect. And your mouth and tongue have a very acute sense of touch, so use that too for your advantage.

Here's the prime point: Especially while you're on my diet (which is not forever), *get the greatest enjoyment from every bit of food and drink you ingest.* For that accomplishment, employ your sense of touch. Deliberately touch-feel the crispness of a celery stalk, the resilience of a cherry tomato, the springiness of a mushroom cap, and so with all the foods you touch.

When your tongue touches food, think specifically of its consistency—hard, soft, moist. Test the temperature—hot, cold, lukewarm. Pay full attention; *eat and chew slowly* to get the most enjoyment of texture from every bite, each sip. Thus, aided by all the variations of touch and touch-feel, you'll get utmost gratification from the nutritious and delicious food on your DeBetz Diet.

SEE AND PERCEIVE

The sense of *seeing* coupled with *perceiving* can help you enjoy your food to the utmost as you diet. Perceiving goes beyond just sight; as described in the dictionary, it is "to become aware of by means of the senses, to understand or form an idea of." That means applying more intelligent thinking about food, in addition to utilizing the other senses beneficially in eating.

Use the STOPlines that are part of your support procedure, and look at your food as you ask yourself silently, "How hungry am I right now?" "How much have I eaten so far today?" "What am I going to eat for the rest of the day?" By examining the food you are about to eat in relation to the rest of your day's eating, you'll enjoy every bit to the maximum.

Add the extra pleasure of *seeing* and examining each serving— how everything is arranged on the plate, color combinations, textures. In some cultures, such as Japan, this appearance aspect of eating is developed especially, for good reason. The amounts are usually small, but the arrangements of colorful vegetables, glistening little amounts of meat, fish, herbs, even flowers for decoration, are so appealing that the eating is most satisfying, regardless of the amount.

If you have any doubt about the value to you of seeing and perceiving what you eat, note this dramatic fact: Experiments at a noted institution proved that people have less of an appetite, and eat less, if the visual component is eliminated, with all the food presented equally. How could this be done?

The scientists liquefied all the food—pizza in one test. The resulting thick substance was spooned into a wide-mouthed bottle and offered as dinner. Even though the glass container was labeled "Pizza," the eaters didn't enjoy it, since the visual appeal was missing. ("That gook ain't pizza!")

The same result was repeated with various foods and different individuals involved. When the visual appeal was absent, so was the eating enjoyment. The lesson is obvious: Look at your food on the diet, and always. Perceive all its visual delights. Feast with your eyes as well as your other senses, and you've gone a long way to enjoying and benefiting most in your diet eating.

UTILIZE YOUR SENSE OF SMELL

As a gourmet, "a connoisseur of fine food and drink," you'll use your sense of smell fully to enjoy what you eat on the diet, and after you've trimmed to your desired weight. While appreciating the sight of your food, utilize your sense of smell. Inhale the fragrance of hot and cold foods, enhanced by seasonings, spices, herbs.

Actually, human taste buds can distinguish among only four different tastes: sweet, sour, bitter, and salty. Everything else is transmitted through the sense of smell. So make the most of your olfactory capabilities.

Considered scientifically, the nuances of smells are being transmitted through your nose into the limbic system of the brain, where certain pleasurable (as well as other) associations and memories are recalled. Thus, smell and memory are closely allied; isn't that true in your experience? All the more reason to take your time and allow the fragrance of the food to delight you.

Remember the wonderful smell of the Thanksgiving turkey sizzling in the oven? (Remove the skin before eating!) That's associated, courtesy of your limbic system, with good times with family and friends. On the other hand, when you had a cold, which stifled your sense of smell, your appetite too was submerged. To get the most from your food when dieting, utilize your sense of smell to the maximum.

A recent event at which I was present dramatized the essential involvement of the sense of smell in the enjoyment of food: At a sumptuous buffet where most people were overloading their plates, a slim, handsome gentleman was eating sparingly. Asked how he was able to be so controlled, he sighed. "Everything tastes the same to me, always bland. Unfortunately, I inherited a family trait—I have no sense of smell. It's far greater an affliction than you would imagine." Think of that, and use the conclusion in a positive way. Inhale the fragrance and savor tasteful eating as a delightful part of living—kept within bounds.

When I related the buffet incident to a newly slim patient, she nodded appreciatively. "I'd much rather stay slim with touch-control than by blocking off and losing my sense of smell." Wouldn't you too rather just touch to stop overeating? Noted epicure Brillat-Savarin, who extolled the fragrance of fine food as part of eating, also said, "He who eats too much knows not *how* to eat."

UNDERSTAND TASTE TO BE TRIM

When you take the time to taste and relish each bit of food, you can get far more pleasure from savoring a small portion than from gulping huge mouthfuls. Realize that you taste anything only while it is in your mouth, actually on your tongue. Once it is swallowed, your stomach can't differentiate and appreciate the tastes of whatever comes down. That's right—your stomach doesn't know whether you swallowed chopped spinach or a chocolate ice-cream sundae.

Your stomach's function is not to taste but to break down the intake into its nutritional components—protein, fat, carbohydrates, vitamins, minerals, fiber, and such. Knowing this, you'll want to make the taste experience total before you shuttle the food into your stomach. Eat slowly; chew thoroughly to get the most taste, so that even the smallest amounts satisfy.

The thrilling change that can be yours was described vividly by a patient, Col. Bruce R. Concannon, 56. He took off 25 pounds through touch-control and diet, and said, "I feel and look like a million—make that a billion—again wearing the same size uniform as 30 years ago. The biggest surprise is that I eat less, but enjoy it more. Before I was swallowing without tasting. Now I get pleasure from the taste and also the aroma and texture as I chew slowly. My wife says she actually likes cooking since I'm appreciative instead of gulping food like it was slop. And the best news, all my youthful vigor—well, almost all—is back."

ATTENTION ON DIGESTION

Too many people don't understand or pay enough attention to factors of digestion when dieting, or to general eating and good health. It's valuable to focus on promoting proper digestion in your system. Realize first that the mouth is stage one in the digestive process, making it essential that you chew your food well.

A woman with a particular problem, Mathilda Stedman, 76, was referred to me by her physician regarding a rather unusual complexity, aside from her overweight. As she explained, "I hate my dentures because I gag every time I try to fit them in. I rarely wear them, so when I eat I don't chew."

Because she didn't chew her food, she had developed digestive stomach and gallbladder troubles. Her doctor said he hoped I could help her relax herself and her throat so she'd be able to wear her dentures without gagging. After two sessions, she could do so. When she was able to chew, her digestive problems disappeared quickly. Then, through my diet combined with touch-control, she took off her burdensome overweight. This is just one more illustration of how chewing and digesting properly are very important, can even be crucial in affecting total health.

What happens organically as you eat is that the food in your mouth gets mixed with saliva. When you chew thoroughly, more volume goes down into your stomach—but less food. This probably sounds self-contradictory, but it's worth taking a minute to realize what happens. Try this little experiment, which I often ask patients to do:

Take two pieces of hard cheese of the same size. Put one piece in your mouth, bite it once or twice, and quickly swallow it. Now put the second piece in your mouth and chew it thoroughly for about 15 seconds. Before swallowing it, stop and note that it feels like a little airy ball in your mouth.

What happens organically when the second piece, which you

chewed well, descends into your stomach is that it is greater in volume because it is well mixed with saliva. The first piece is far less in volume, much denser in food, since it hasn't been enlarged with lots of saliva. Here's the result: Once your stomach is filled to a certain level, it transmits a signal to the brain that you are full and feel satiated, that you've *had enough and should stop eating.*

Clearly, the more you chew, the greater the volume, and the less food is in your stomach. As a result, by chewing more, you feel full with less food. Try to assess this consciously a few times when you eat, and you'll be convinced (if you're not already) and will agree that you should chew, chew, chew, and then chew again. It will help your digestion and accelerate your weight-loss progress.

RECOGNIZE EMOTIONAL VERSUS PHYSICAL HUNGER

Once you recognize the difference between emotional and physical hunger—which I seek to clarify for you with specific facts throughout this book—you will have gone a long way toward effective lifelong weight control. You can eliminate "emotional" eating—that is, blaming your "hunger" on your frustrations—and instead eat for nutrition to feed your body's true physical hunger. By using my stop and support methods to help keep your emotional demands in check, you too will find yourself responding only to your physical needs. You'll be bolstered by your steady weight loss, and ultimately by your slimmed, more attractive appearance and feeling of vibrant health.

Your trim, attractive body will become so gratifying to you that you won't allow yourself to eat for emotional reasons—anger, frustration, stress, boredom, other negatives. You will become increasingly and definitely aware of the differences between an emotional appetite and actual physical hunger. Always, you'll have the stop and support systems at your fingertips to help you stay trim year after year.

The big difference between before and now is that now you not only "think thin" but you have the touch method, the action tool to ward off temptation and to keep extra pounds from creeping up. You can assure yourself with profound relief: "I'll never be heavy again."

Here are some extra specific aids to use in addition to repeated application of your stop and support action tools. These innovations have worked for my patients throughout my medical practice:

First, set up a list of alternatives to turn to when you are tempted by emotional hunger (called "alternative coping mechanism" professionally). Select from what best accords with your personal likes and life-style. These "instead ofs" have been effective for others: Exercise to relieve tensions. Take a warm bath. Call a friend. Play your favorite records. Write letters you've been putting off. Read. Watch a movie or TV. Drink a Touch Highball (seltzer, lemon slice, plus a little no-calorie sweetener if you like).

Make up your own list of alternatives, and use one or more if diet-breaking tempts you. It's simple—instead of eating, *do something else*. If you think you must keep your mouth busy, munch any of the long list of permitted snacks in chapter 4. Or sip a Touch Highball as you read an absorbing book, magazine, or newspaper. One formerly overweight patient, a computer addict, said that her alternative, poring over computer manuals, fed her mind instead of overfeeding her body. What's your preference?

Another effective instruction: Make it a rule *not to do something else while eating*, such as watching TV or reading or writing. Now that eating has taken a different meaning in your life, make sure that while you eat within stay-trim limits, you fully *enjoy* what you eat. If your attention is distracted, and you don't pay full attention to eating, you won't be aware of what and how much you eat, or of your body's signal that you've had enough. Concentrate on getting the greatest enjoyment from every permissible calorie—then stop.

YOU CAN SAY "NO"

You may recall the song lament of the oversexed young woman who wailed, "I cain't say no." I urge the conviction in

you that from now on you can and will say "No!" about overeating. If you find yourself pressured to eat, remember: "Touch"
and "No" to a hostess or anyone else pushing you to eat more.
No! In restaurants or at a dinner party, evaluate the amount of
food on your plate, and if it's too much for your diet or stay-
trim program—no!

Keep in mind that a restaurant dishes out the same amount of
food to a 5'2" sedentary secretary as to a 6'8" muscled football
player. It's up to you to determine how much you need. Wherever you are—even if well-meaning Mom urged you in growing
up, "Finish what's on your plate, there are children starving in
the world"—now you're grown up and can say "No!"

You won't lessen famine in the world by overeating; you'll
just add to your own problem. Consider a wise American Heart
Association ad captioned, "We're Fighting for Your Life." It goes
on: "We take exception to what your mother taught you. You shouldn't eat
everything put in front of you. By cutting down on rich, fatty foods,
you can do yourself a big favor. You could lower your blood
cholesterol level and reduce your risk of heart disease."

FOOD—A REWARD OR BRIBE?

Understanding the basis of much emotional eating can help
you. Unfortunately, like many others in this food-oriented culture, you may have grown up being soothed or rewarded or
bribed with food. Therefore, many associate eating with a vast
range of emotional situations. They attribute to food almost
magical powers to help feel better, happier, stronger, less tired.

Wrong! However you may have been indoctrinated in your
early years, you're an intelligent, self-sustaining adult now. As
such, and particularly as you absorb the information and recommendations in these pages, you'll know this: Basically the
function of food is for nutrition, to feed the body hunger—and
not to assuage emotional frustrations.

It's psychological fact that there was just one period in life
when food really functioned to relieve tension as well as hunger
—that was in infancy. An infant's primary needs are to be warm,
safe, and fed. When an infant is hungry, her (or his) nervous

system gets "frustrated." She gets tense, starts crying vehemently. As soon as she's held and fed by breast or bottle, she starts to feel comfortable and happy.

That was the origin of the development of this age-old response to eat when frustrated or tense. Digest this potent fact thoroughly: For the infant, physical hunger was the cause of the frustration—therefore food could alleviate it. But for grown-ups, the frustration is usually caused not by physical hunger. It's because the boss yelled at you, or that all-important person didn't call back, or other negative pressures.

Nevertheless, a common tendency is to turn back to a mechanism—eating—that early in life relieved the frustration, anxiety, and tension, *but not anymore*. Such relief is short-lived because the cause of the tension is something other than hunger. Think about it—understanding this can help you tremendously.

Moreover, equipped with your touch-control action tool, you have a further aid to relieve the uncomfortable feeling of being tense, anxious, or frustrated in more adult and mature ways—rather than by destructive overeating. Again, use the 20-second stop action—a pressure reliever in this instance: Touch, relax, repeat the three reminder STOPlines. That's sure 20-second relief every time.

Reviewing this chapter and all the preceding, you can be sure that you're on your way to transforming yourself into being a thin eater rather than a fat eater lifelong ("permanent internalized change"). A thin eater, one who makes choices intelligently based on physical rather than emotional hunger, is a true gourmet. You'll enjoy every aspect of eating, benefiting fully from these senses: touch-feel, sight-perception, smell, and taste, aided by knowledge about digestion and good sense in utilizing your senses deliberately.

9

HOW-TO EXAMPLES FROM MY PATIENT CASEBOOK

Records of Steady Healthful Weight Loss

All these typical condensed case reports provide you with self-help information for your guidance. They spotlight specific problems and experiences of others as lessons from which you can profit. The individuals covered here, as well as innumerable others, reduced successfully in spite of past failures. *So can you.*

As with the case histories throughout this book, accounts are based on my notes made in consultations with a wide variety of women and men in my day-to-day medical practice. As with the cases cited in previous chapters, all names have been altered to protect the privacy of the individuals. The experiences of several patients may be combined in some of these reports so that no one person could be identified.

"RICH FOOD WAS MY REWARD"

Gail Weylinde, realtor, 44, 5'4", 153 pounds, goal 125. "I was a heavy child, but as an adult I managed to maintain a weight of about 133 until the past two years. Putting in long, hard days at the office and driving people around, I got into the habit of rewarding myself before dinner. I'd have a couple of martinis and fattening hors d'oeuvres like hot melted cheese on buttered biscuits, pigs in blankets, all that rich stuff. When I topped 150, my boss started hinting that being fat as a house was a hindrance to showing houses to some customers. Some 'reward'!" She was close to tears.

After she'd dropped 28 pounds and reached her 125-pound goal, she said, "When you impressed on me that the real reward in food is nutrition and good health for my body and I learned to respect my body, that was the turning point. Dr. DeBetz, your three 'body' STOPlines saved me every time from breaking my diet. The other day my husband and teenage daughter caught me admiring my body in the full-length mirror. They *applauded*. That's my greatest reward."

"MY DOWNFALL—HUGE FAMILY MEALS"

Dr. Simeon Hendleman, dental surgeon, 33, 6'2", 242 pounds, goal 195. "My wife, pregnant with our first child, became worried about my health because I'm so overweight. I checked with my doctor, who referred me to you because I have a triple problem: I love to eat. I eat huge family meals, especially each Friday Sabbath, since we're orthodox. Both my parents are heavy, so there's a heredity factor. Can you help me?"

Dr. Hendleman's blood pressure was up. He lacked stamina and was short of breath, due primarily to being almost 50 pounds overweight. "All diets have failed me," he sighed. "I joined one of those nationwide reducing groups, but it was no help to me." When I explained my methods he said, "I'm dubious, but I'll give it a try."

An intelligent man, he used my diet with touch-control and lost considerable weight from the first day. Employing the stop and support procedures faithfully, he stopped eating when full, even at Sabbath dinners. He said, "I soon hated the feeling of being overfull. To my surprise, I found much greater pleasure in savoring my food slowly like a gourmet, instead of swallowing rapidly and overeating."

Reaching his goal of 195 pounds, he enthused, "I not only

unloaded the fat that was making me sick, but I lost incredible inches all over my body. I used to push my big body around like an elephant, now I move freely. I thank you, my wife thanks you."

"Wonderful," I answered. "A friend recently said that even the Talmud warns against overweight: 'In eating, a third of the stomach should be filled with food, a third with drink, and the rest left empty.' "

Dr. Hendleman smiled. "I'll quote that ancient wisdom to my mother, especially when she starts urging me to eat more food on the Sabbath. Obviously, as with just about everything, moderation is the key."

"ASHAMED OF SHOWING MY BODY"

Peggy Johnson, restaurant assistant manager, 23, 5'4", 144 pounds, goal 125. "I came to the big city three years ago to make my fortune," she explained, her handsome face twisted in a frown. "As a black woman, I felt that I had to work twice as hard to prove my ability. Surrounded by food all the time, I got fat. I know that being overweight isn't good for my career, but even more important, I want to get married soon. Though my future husband doesn't mind my being 20 pounds overweight, I'm ashamed of showing my flabby body. No matter how many diets I've tried, I haven't been able to reduce."

I was happy to help. Peggy Johnson was like many who find their overweight interfering with romance. With my diet and touch methods, she started losing weight week by week. Then suddenly she moved back to Georgia. I lost track of her until she called after almost three years.

"On your diet," she said, "I'd touch and say the stop and support lines without fail—and I still do when needed. I went right down to 120 pounds, and am still there, although I'm still in the restaurant business. I'm happily married and pregnant. But I'm sure I'll get thin again after the baby comes, because I know how. I had to phone to thank you."

"I'm delighted," I told her, "but no thanks needed. I just showed you the way, then you did it yourself." I must stress again—I can't diet or touch for you; you have to do it yourself.

"BUSINESS DINNERS DID ME IN"

Anthony Piccarra, building contractor, 38, 5'11", 210 pounds, goal 175. He expressed a common problem. "For my business, I have to entertain at a lot of dinners as well as lunches. I got in the habit of eating big and knocking off at least a bottle of wine myself to encourage clients to dine and drink lavishly. Now I'm way out of shape, and I have terrible indigestion. For my own sake and for my wife and three kids, I must drop to 175 pounds, as I was in college."

I learned that his parents and brothers were all overweight, but that his wife, who had been a heavy child, had become very nutrition-conscious and made sure that none of their three youngsters were heavy. I pointed out to Mr. Piccarra that his heredity obviously should not be a bar to his losing weight. He interjected, "I golf every weekend—that should help me lose weight." I explained that golf is fine recreation but that no activity or exercise uses enough calories if you overeat (see chapter 10).

I provided him with the DeBetz Diet, taught him my touch-control techniques, and asked him to phone in a month. He called enthusiastically. "I'm eating and drinking like a gourmet, as you suggested. No more drinking wine by the bottle. I enjoy sipping the one glass of dry wine permitted on the diet more than swilling down a whole bottle."

He added proudly, "At a business dinner last night, I drank an espresso instead of having the zabaglione [a creamy Italian dessert] I ordered for my guests. None of them minded. I've dropped pounds and inches each week. No more indigestion. And," triumphantly, "I've cut six strokes from my golf score." I don't guarantee that.

"SNACKING PUT ON THE POUNDS"

Harry P. McNeill, journalist, 32, 5'9", 195 pounds, goal 160. He told me glumly, "Seeing my bulging body now, you'd never know I was a star athlete in college. I never had to watch what I ate. But soon after graduation I fell on the ice, smashed my shoulder, had to say good-bye to strenuous sports. Out of boredom and frustration, I started gorging and chain-smoking like there was no tomorrow. I gained 10 pounds, 20, then 30. Gave up cigarettes a couple of weeks ago and I'm swelling like a blimp."

I asked about his eating habits.

"Snacking did me in. I'm out of my newspaper cubbyhole most of the day, doing interviews, covering stories, eating haphazardly. I grab a beer and pretzels here, a hot dog there, another beer with cheese and crackers. I've tried and fallen off two diets in the last month. One of the guys said you took off his weight, and he looks terrific. My doctor is concerned and told me I have to reduce because my blood pressure is going up rapidly."

First I assured him that giving up smoking need not make him gain weight and I could help him there too. He said, "Good, that's a step forward. As for eating, I know I have an oral fixation due to feeling deprived as a kid because my mother favored my older brother. I sucked my thumb until I was 13, and grabbed snacks all day as compensation for feeling neglected."

"Nevertheless," I assured him, "you'll be able to stop snacking with the touch-control procedures. You'll touch and stop. You'll control your eating instead of the snacking habit controlling you."

He responded well and lost weight steadily. He reported, "I enjoy social dinners now, though I used to avoid them because I was afraid they meant pig-out time for me. And no more snacking and grabbing food on the run—if I'm tempted, I simply touch and stop."

Here's a good example of the proved fact that learning restraint, knowing the procedures that promote low-calorie eating, and following the right balanced diet can result in trimness and good health. That's true whatever the obstacles and temptations may be.

"MOTHERHOOD MADE ME FAT"

Sheila Matthews, homemaker, 37, 5'4", 205 pounds, goal 130–135. "I've figured out," this big, appealing woman told me, "that motherhood and running a family and home made me overeat terribly. I've always had a weight problem, but managed to have a passable figure at 140 pounds when I married, 16 years ago. Now, with three kids always on the go, my husband running a big business and away a lot, I eat meals with the kids. Then I finish what they leave on their plates—I hate waste." She looked despairing.

"Cooking, shopping, cleaning up, I'm so knocked out at night that I collapse into bed after dinner. I watch TV, eating potato chips, peanuts, cheese, and other fattening stuff. Six months ago my husband had a heart attack, and the doctor made him slim down. He warned that I was headed for a heart attack too unless I take off 50 pounds."

I've found that many women blame their overweight on trying to alleviate the undeniable pressures of raising a family and running a home. Telling them just to diet and eat less doesn't work. As I've stated, I realized long ago that overweights need a specific physical-emotional action aid in addition to a low-calorie balanced diet. So I developed the touch-control method to provide personal self-control.

Like others, Mrs. Matthews was finally able to reduce based on my two-way method and her own resolve. She told me after several months, "I was doubtful that a touch could overcome the pressures that haven't let up. But your system worked, as you can see. I'm 50 pounds lighter and incredibly healthier and happier. I'm following your lifelong blueprint and keeping my weight just where I want it. I'm not skinny, but have an attractive body again."

"FAT PARENTS, FAT KID—
I COULDN'T BE SLIM"

Martin T. Drexler, stockbroker, 45, 6'1", 250 pounds, goal 199. This gentleman is a prime example of why many overweight individuals give up hope of being slim, graceful, and athletic—due to their background. "I had very fat parents," this patient said, "was a fat kid, and I was sure that I couldn't ever be thin. Plus, in my frenzied business I compensated by eating huge amounts. I failed in two marriages, at least partly due to being so fat and clumsy. Yeah, even sex was difficult."

He brightened. "My third marriage has lasted eight years. She's a beautiful, wonderful woman. But I'm so damned flabby and unhealthy, I'm afraid I'll lose her. I ran into a college chum last week who used to be even fatter than me and now is trim and amazingly young-looking—thanks to your help, he said. Your 'touch' method sounds weird to me, but I'm ready to give it a shot."

"Try to listen without prejudice," I said. "Understand first that touch-control alone won't do it. What works is the combination with my diet and *your total cooperation.* It's not true that you can't slim down because your whole family was heavy."

Eager to slim down, Mr. Drexler at last had the will and the way to succeed. Losing pounds week after week, he transformed into a trim, attractive gourmet at his 199-pound goal. It's a bonus to me that he has maintained his "under 200" weight for years, and has referred to me many friends and associates who also succeeded with my guidance.

"I WAS ASHAMED WHEN I ENTERED
COLLEGE"

Suzi Beleye, college student, 20, 5'5", 154 pounds, goal 125. This bright young woman came to see me soon after she had started her first year at a large university. She sat slumped and dejected as she said, "I've always had a weight problem. I was a chubby child, and it never bothered me much because my mother is fat so I thought that's how it had to be. Now that I'm in college, surrounded by so many beautiful, thin classmates, I'm ashamed of myself."

She looked up with a half-smile. "I don't want to look like a skinny rock star, just normal. I've got to take of 25 to 30 pounds. I've tried a few diets, but they don't do it; they don't stop me from snacking and overeating. A psychology student told me you'd developed a reducing program with something extra, some kind of a 'touching' system. Well, it sounds odd, but I'm ready to try anything. I must get thin like the others."

That extra touch, my action tool, turned out to be just what Suzi needed. It kept her on my diet without snacking or over-eating. She lost weight steadily, and her spirits rose as the pounds came off. After she reached her goal, she insisted that her mother come to see me. She slimmed down too, week by week, even though she said at the start, "I can't remember when I wasn't overweight. I thought there was no way I could lose weight. But my Suzi said if she could do it, I could too." She could and did.

"EXAMPLE IS THE SCHOOL OF MANKIND . . ."

It's my hope and belief that you will learn and benefit from noting these few examples of individuals who overcame various blind spots. With new insight and aid, they finally reached their weight-loss and weight-control goals, just as you can.

These individuals, as you realize from their brief stories, are not supermen or superwomen. They used the same dieting and touch-control procedures, along with my other specific and general recommendations provided for you throughout this book. I can't repeat too often, in order to impress on you deeply enough, that *these methods can work for you if you'll work with them*— not overnight, but over a reasonable period of time.

10
YOUR PERSONAL ACTIVITY PROGRAM

Teamed with the DeBetz Diet and Touch-Control

"I hate exercise!" Even if you're someone who has always said that in the past, you'll learn here how to get the benefits and even enjoyment from effective body movement as part of your lifelong weight-control program. Many trim, healthy, formerly overweight patients have obtained that enduring reward with my methods.

First, you'll be pleased to find that my attitude and instructions about exercise are different. I'm concerned fundamentally about productive movement, not muscle-building. Based on my medical and psychological training and practice, and successful experience with so many overweight women and men, I don't state that you *must* exercise in order to lose excess weight. Nor do I insist on specific strenuous physical routines as part of your reducing program.

My recommendations to you take a much different approach. As you know by now, my methods are based strongly on instilling in you a sense of responsibility for your body. Working closely with you now, I don't tell you to exercise just for the sake of exercising, because "it's good for you." I want you to concentrate on your body itself as an entity, with this very personal thinking approach:

You know that your body consists of internal organs, bones, muscles, tendons, and so on. To keep your body functioning most efficiently and healthfully you must fulfill the fundamental needs of all your organs and elements. One obvious way is to feed your body properly, as taught here. Another necessity for top performance of each part is to keep your body active. You'll not only look and feel better, you'll move better. You owe your body this special care, don't you?

Realize then that activity is essential. Your bones, muscles, and joints need to be moved in many different directions. Your muscles require being stretched and flexed. It's just good sense to face the physical facts of daily living. You've experienced the result of prolonged sitting or standing or lying or crouching in one position, whether at a desk or table or anywhere. It makes your body feel stiff and "frozen," almost immobilized, at least partially.

We've all suffered that uncomfortable sensation of being "locked" into a position, even if temporarily. To avoid such impairment even as a fleeting warning, your body needs to be kept reasonably active. That's true not just for the primary purpose of helping to lose weight, but also to avoid the loss of some body function and to ward off the onset of body deterioration. You certainly are not going to let your body run down like an unwound clock when the right activity can keep it running properly.

WHAT ACTIVITY IS RIGHT FOR YOU?

As the first step, you now recognize and agree about the need for keeping your body active. The next step is to decide what activity will promote your physical fitness best from the one viewpoint that is absolutely vital: What would you personally welcome and enjoy most?

It would be ridiculous to recommend and demand torturous gymnastics or heavy weight lifting or strenuous jogging of a 30- or 60-year-old woman or man who abhors overexertion. As you know, that's what is actually urged by some zealots. Instead, sit back and give some thought to your personal activity choice.

Right now, apply your enhanced peak-concentration ability, using the touch-control technique, to focus on selecting one or more activities that suit you best. Try this pleasant concentration routine: In privacy, sit down and relax. Look up and close your eyes as you touch your face (your concentration signal). With your eyes closed, and with your finger touching any part of your face comfortably, take a few restful moments to think about your personal preference in physical activity.

As you focus your thinking and run down the list of activities readily available to you, you'll find that your body will start telling you what physical movement it likes, ranging from the least to the most demanding. There are many good conditioning activities to consider.

Would your body enjoy walking, swimming, bicycling, dancing, various competitive and team sports? Remember that the vital point is to choose what you think is right for you, regardless of someone else's preference. By pinpointing your personal likes and dislikes, you won't be talked into anything you don't want, or even hate. But you must move your body lest vital parts waste away, just as you don't want excess fat to impede the normal functioning of your internal and external organs.

If you have no strong preferences, here are some excellent activities to mull over: If you are considerably overweight, the safest kind of body motion is brisk walking. That's a very healthful activity at any weight, recommended by doctors and other experts universally. Brisk, continuous walking activates and helps your bones, joints, muscles, heart, and lungs. Also, there are obvious emotional benefits in getting out, moving your body, breathing in the air, appreciating your surroundings consciously. Consider walking in place with brisk movements indoors, too.

No, you don't have to walk tens of miles, or adopt exaggerated motions as in race walking. You don't need any special clothing, space, or tools. Walking briskly for 20 minutes daily is all you usually need to get started, the same for walking in place —using an exercise treadmill if desired, perhaps in front of a TV set indoors. Use your lunch hour, or take a break at any time of morning, afternoon, or evening, or get off the bus two miles from work and walk the rest of the way. Analyze and allocate your own special times. With proper walking shoes (not anything like towering spike heels, of course), you should be safe from injuries or harm to your body.

Sustained swimming is another excellent activity for your body. It's also one of the safest forms of exercising, since it doesn't exert excessive stress on weight-bearing joints or on your spine or entire frame. You can usually locate a nearby pool at a school or club or Y. Learn smooth-flowing action and keep at it lap after lap. This provides superb conditioning, as hopping in and out of the water cannot.

Bicycling offers healthful exercise when done in a sustained way with smooth, comfortable exertion. Stop-and-start won't do much for your body. You must keep your legs moving so that your muscles can pump blood steadily. That's exhilarating fun as well as excellent movement.

If you have any concern at all about any specific activity, ask for your doctor's permission. If walking or swimming or bicycling doesn't suit you or is impractical for you, select from the list of activities that follows shortly. Above all, if you're a motivated individual, you need only look around your area, read local newspapers with an eye to readily available activities and facilities, and arrange to get fullest advantage from them. Before you start *any* exercise program, particularly if you have been sedentary, you should check with your doctor to make sure that you are fit to start on a physical activity program.

THE REWARDS OF ACTIVITY FOR WEIGHT LOSS

First, I must clarify further the very real emotional benefits of activity. It's now quite accepted that there's a physical-organic reason why you feel good emotionally when you engage in physical activity. That includes brisk walking, swimming, bicycling, jogging, running, practically any exertion. Your brain produces endorphins, substances that act to block out pain, and also tend to make you feel good, elevating your spirits, too.

In terms of reducing, it's true that exercise burns some calories, and if done on a regular basis will contribute to weight loss. However, realistically, the effect on overweight for the average person is limited so far as calorie reduction goes. There are additional benefits of regular and sufficient activity and exercise, but to reduce effectively, physical exertion must be linked to an effective weight-loss diet.

It's agreed by all but some overzealous exponents that exercise alone can't be counted on to take off excess pounds in most people. Nevertheless, I recommend activity for the many stated reasons. To assess calorie loss through exercise and activity, I suggest that you note the following calorie expenditure listing. As one realistic scientist said, "I'm a jogger for many reasons. But so far as taking off pounds goes, I could jog for a half-hour, then eat a four-inch wedge of watermelon, for instance, and all the lost calories would be back."

Nobody can assess exactly the loss of calories from exercise. Obviously, there are too many variables in size and makeup of the individuals involved, speed, and many other considerations. The following listing is a consensus, based on a number of authoritative findings and tables. If your activity isn't listed, you can arrive at a general figure by comparing it with the other exertions.

BONUS BENEFITS FROM SUSTAINED ACTIVITY

Sustained action in whatever activity you choose is necessary to get the full available rewards. If in walking, for example, you just saunter along, stopping to chat, you get enjoyment but you're not really exercising your body much. In bicycling, if you dawdle along slowly, stop to look around, then go on again, your body is hardly getting a workout. Again, don't delude yourself—move and keep moving.

Probably more important than burning off calories, exercise increases your metabolic rate (relating to expenditure of energy). Even after you have stopped the sustained activity, the increased metabolic rate stays up for a while, continuing to burn off some extra calories.

Also, due to the release of endorphins (substances that are released in the brain) that have been mobilized during the exercise, these continue to circulate in your blood to some extent

APPROXIMATE CALORIES USED IN A HALF-HOUR

Activity	120-lb. Woman	160-lb. Man
Bicycling, sustained	200–300	300–400
Calisthenics (depends on exertion)	140–250	180–350
Canoeing	100–150	130–180
Carpentry, workbench	120–140	140–180
Climbing stairs	130–160	160–190
Dancing, moderate	100–130	130–170
Dancing, energetic	200–400	250–500
Fencing	110–130	130–160
Football	250–300	300–400
Gardening, active	120–140	140–180
Golf, riding cart	70–90	80–100
Golf, without cart	100–140	140–180
Handball	200–350	300–400
Hockey, field, ice	250–300	300–400
Horseback riding, active	140–160	160–200
Housework, general, active	80–130	110–160
Jogging, average	200–250	250–300
Karate	320–350	360–400
Lacrosse	250–300	350–400
Lawn mowing, hand	100–130	130–150
Office work, active	70–130	90–150
Piano playing	80–130	100–150
Rowing, vigorous	300–400	400–500
Running	300–400	400–500
Skating, ice, roller, energetic	200–300	250–350
Skiing, energetic	200–300	250–350
Square dancing	140–160	160–180
Soccer	250–300	350–400
Squash	180–240	250–400
Swimming, sustained	200–300	300–400
Table tennis	150–180	200–250
Tennis, recreational	180–220	250–280
Violin playing	70–100	90–130
Volleyball	180–220	220–280
Walking, brisk	140–160	160–180
Water skiing	210–230	230–250

and actually act to suppress your appetite. Haven't you noticed that when you exericise energetically you don't feel hungry at all immediately afterward? You might be thirsty, but hardly very hungry, so it does tend to reduce your eating.

Another valuable aspect of physical activity is that it is excellent in helping to get rid of tension. As revealed in a number of the earlier case histories, overweights often admit, "I have to eat to get rid of stress, frustration, anxiety, and a pileup of pressures. Food becomes my tension reliever." I assure you that from every aspect of my experience as a physician and psychiatrist, physical activity is far more effective to help alleviate the unpleasant sensations of tension than a hot butterscotch sundae ever could be.

EXERCISE MODERATION IN EXERCISING

Abandonment of moderation was emphasized as a modern health menace at a symposium on diet and exercise of the American Medical Association, Council on Scientific Affairs. In addition to the "immoderate habits," eating rich foods, overeating, and other bad eating habits, the report stressed the health importance of weight control coupling proper diet and physical activity. I agree totally, and spell out for you in detail the how-tos throughout this book. Again—do, but don't overdo.

Body composition was also underscored in the symposium. That means relating ideal weight in pounds to lean body tissue, skeletal mass, and energy stores, for maximum health. I urge you to keep this all-important linkage in mind always. Thus, physical activity and exercise, along with proper eating for weight control, will add enjoyment in living for you from now on, fitting in with your new concept of body awareness.

To make sure that you keep your commitment and take fullest advantage of physical movement, integrating it with your diet thoroughly, try this pleasant touch-control activity a few times every day:

Sit comfortably. Relax your mind and entire body as you look upward, touch your face as usual, and close your eyes. In privacy, either think silently or say aloud these three ACTIVlines:

For my body, joints, bones, and muscles, inactivity
is an insult and neglects my physical needs.
I need my entire body and all organs at their fittest
for my best health and appearance.
I owe it to my body to exercise regularly.

Start today to choose your prime physical activity. Use your
three touch-control ACTIVlines regularly. Your double reward
will be your steady weight loss plus increased energy and grace
of movement. Day by day you'll become more aware of the
benefits to your body and to your emotional well-being. And
you'll be exercising with pleasure rather than regarding physical
activity as a task or a chore.

"IT SHOULD HAPPEN TO A DOG..."

In a typical instance of a person who "hates exercise," a busy
decorator, Daphne Lassiter, 29, was extremely inactive physically. As much as possible, she resisted leaving her office in her
luxurious apartment. Although she was losing pounds consistently through touch-control and my diet, I was concerned
about her lethargy. I had an idea as she talked about her little
dog, Chloe, who was walked twice a day by a dog-tending service.

I asked why she used the service, and she responded instantly,
"Chloe needs to run and play. She's only two years old and
loves to scamper outdoors. It would be cruel of me not to
provide her with what she needs so much."

"What about you?" I asked. "Don't you think your body needs
activity too? Don't you realize that your bones and muscles need
to move and bend and stretch actively?"

"Not my aching bones! I'm glad to settle at my desk to work,
and then to just sit around and watch TV at the end of the day."

"Your bones ache because you won't listen to your body, as
I've recommended," I said. "You ache because your bones and
muscles, your whole body wants to move and function and

respond to real activity, as nature intended. You see the need so clearly for your dog, why not for yourself? Instead of hiring others, how about walking Chloe outdoors yourself? See how you feel after one week of that. I prescribe that, for the benefit of you and your dog."

She smiled. "You're the doctor—I'll try it." A few days later she admitted that she was enjoying the outdoor activity. Not long afterward she terminated the dog service altogether. Needless to say, she lost even more pounds and inches with the enjoyable activity added, and was even more lively and lovely.

PEOPLE LIVE LONGER . . . ACTIVELY

"Study Indicates Moderate Exercise Can Add Years to a Person's Life"—that's a recent *New York Times* headline. The news story explains: "A continuing study of nearly 17,000 Harvard alumni has demonstrated that moderate physical exercise in adult life can significantly increase life expectancy." As reported in the *New England Journal of Medicine*, the study's participants engaged in such activities as walking, stair climbing, and sports. They used 2,000 calories or more a week, on average, equivalent to walking briskly only about three miles a day. Their death rates were *one-quarter to one-third lower* than of people in the study who were least active. Indications are that the results would probably apply to women as well as men.

The individuals in this study, covering 16 years to date, are not necessarily athletes, just active people. The conclusions are significant for you, as they suggest that "exercise in and of itself is protective."

"YOUR MUSCLE TONE HAS IMPROVED DRAMATICALLY"

Here's more proof of the value of activity in promoting allover health and keeping weight down to where you want it. Samm Sinclair Baker, who has coauthored three popular activity-exercise books with noted specialists, suggests specific helps from his personal experience:

"As a pudgy teenager in high school, I longed to get down to normal weight. A smart gym teacher told me that I must change my eating habits, and also become more active. I slimmed down, and have stayed trim since. I watch my diet and make it a point to walk briskly ten miles daily this way: Commuting, I walk the two miles to the train and back, rather than drive. In the city, I walk the two miles to and from the station to the office. For meetings within two miles, I'd walk instead of taking taxis. That's it—walk instead of riding wherever possible.

"When I turned to full-time writing, I bought an exercise bicycle. Our family doctor, calling on my wife, stopped and stared at the exerciser between the twin beds and asked, 'What's that crazy contraption?' I explained that I exercised on it for 20 minutes before breakfast and dinner. He sighed and left.

"A few months later, during my annual checkup, he said in surprise, 'Your muscle tone is terrific since last year's visit —how come?' 'That crazy contraption.' He smiled. 'OK, keep doing what you're doing.' Each year since he has said, 'You're in great shape, keep doing what you're doing.'

"Here's my 'secret' that can mean stay-trim healthier years for you: Put a TV set in front of you as you exercise in 20-minute sessions, indoors—whether it's doing calisthenics or using any apparatus. Watching TV instead of staring into space during your workout, time flies by—no more excuses that 'exercise bores me.' Some individuals to whom I've suggested this react with disgust: 'Me watch TV while I exercise?' Months later: 'Thanks—I'm actually enjoying exercising while watching selected programs. I feel great.' "

WEIGHT-CONTROL AND ACTIVITY CHECKLIST

1. Follow my reducing and weight-control directions faithfully.

2. Select one or more of the fitness activities that suit you best.
3. Exercise regularly, day in and day out, 20 continuous minutes or more, as often as you can. Activity helps you physically and emotionally.
4. Vary activities if you wish—walk one day, swim the next, and so on.
5. Never overexert. Don't try to do more than you can do comfortably. If it hurts or you feel overheated or chilled or dizzy or have any negative symptoms, stop! Don't exercise when you're ill.
6. After you're down to your desired weight and are using my weight-control recommendations, keep active for maximum fitness at every age. The human body begins to deteriorate rapidly if muscles, bones, and joints are not kept moving.
7. Enjoy how your physical activities help you keep vigorous lifelong—physically, mentally, and emotionally.

11

LIFELONG STAY-TRIM BLUEPRINT
An End to Endless Dieting

Keep in mind every day that you have the proved touch-control program going for you from now on as an always available and reliable means of support, physical and emotional. "It's wonderful," newly slim Carol Cooper, 21, told me, "to know that I've reduced and am not then left in the lurch. I'll always have touch-control at my fingertips to help me be free of overweight for the rest of my life. Even though I've been pudgy from my early childhood, I can't even imagine having a weight problem again."

That's true—but only if you never let up in taking care after you're down to your desired weight. You must never forget what you learn in this book about the sure methods for taking off excess pounds and keeping them off. You must follow the stay-trim blueprint here, defined as a "carefully designed plan." Realize again that this blueprint has been carefully developed and perfected during 16 years of medical practice.

I was greatly impressed when my coauthor, Samm Baker, repeated the observation of a noted architect: "Constructed meticulously through knowledge and experience, according to a sound, detailed blueprint, the result is a building that endures." My purpose here is to provide you with a blueprint proved in use by many formerly overweight individuals in my practice. You can follow it confidently to stay trim lifelong. Finally, for you, there's an end to the endless dieting of the past.

Read the details of the following blueprint carefully. I'm sure you will, since I know that you're determined to keep lost pounds from creeping back on you—as probably happened to you before without the support systems you've now learned. Be sure to continue your personally selected daily activity program, too.

First, realize that everything you've been told in the preceding pages applies to staying slim lifelong as well as to reducing—except that you no longer need to stay on the DeBetz Diet day in and day out. Of course, the diet is absolutely essential in order to shed unwanted pounds. But once you're down to where you want to be, you can eat from a wide variety of foods of your choice. Just follow the clear, easy-to-use guidelines here.

Second, never forget that you always have an invaluable aide that you never had before. Now and forever, you have the invaluable touch-control action tool at your fingertips for instant use. You possess the stop and support procedures, and additional information and instructions, to lose weight again, if that's needed, and keep trim.

Third, if, for any reason, you find that unwanted excess weight is coming back, you possess the proved DeBetz Diet, to which you can return. You know you can count on it to take off pounds, since it worked for you before.

Fourth, possessing all these unique supports, you'll be buoyed up by a thrilling lifelong bonus: You'll be able to participate fully, free from fear, in the pleasures of self-controlled gourmet eating from now on. That wasn't possible for you in the past because you didn't have your strong sense of confidence acquired via your new touch-control know-how.

Typically, a former patient, Myra Sidelle, 25, a bright computer programmer, who had been on and off diets all her life, called me when she returned from a luxury cruise: "This was the first time that I felt normal in regard to food. I wasn't frightened by the lavish buffets and captain's dinners or anything else. I just ate deliciously without ever overeating. I never knew how wonderful that felt before, because I was obsessed with food and afraid that I wouldn't know how to handle it. Now that I'm in control, I eat like a normal person—and love it."

YOUR FIVE-POUND RETURN WARNING

This is a must for the first two weeks after you're down to your desired goal and can shift to eating a variety of foods of your choice. Continue to get on the scale every morning before breakfast and weigh yourself unclothed, as you have been doing. That scale is your watchdog, as I've stated before. Seeing the numbers daily is the surest way to know that you're maintaining your weight and not gaining.

After the two-week daily weighing period, you can cut down the morning weigh-in to two or three times a week—although I've found that most of my formerly overweight patients keep on weighing themselves daily. That's a quick and easy procedure which takes only seconds, as you know. It fortifies your assurance every day that you're staying trim—just as you wish. That's your lifelong goal, and you must watch your weight regularly in order to maintain it.

Of course, it's normal for everyone to vary one or a few pounds in weight day to day, due to a variety of factors. Sometimes you'll weigh a pound more than the day before even though you were perfectly controlled and ate moderately. Weight depends primarily on what and how much you eat, but also is affected by hormonal influences such as PMS (premenstrual syndrome), salt consumption, which can cause water retention, and other variables that may occur with both sexes.

So if you didn't overeat and your weight went up a pound, don't be overly concerned. On the other hand, if you overate and yet your weight didn't go up, don't let go and start gorging. Bad eating habits will catch up with you shortly. I can't urge you too strongly to act at once if the five-pound warning number shows on the scale. Recognize the danger and take tight control. Act immediately to take that five pounds off, and use the shock as fair warning not to let a similar weight increase occur again.

Be wary that you don't delude yourself, as happens with some overweights. Don't avoid the telltale scale, as too many people tend to do. In one typical case, Vincent Zimmerman, 45, an office manager, came to see me "because I put on a few extra pounds this year." When I asked how much he weighed, he said, "About 185." I was surprised, because he wasn't tall and appeared very heavy.

When he stepped on my scale, it read 225. Shocked, he said shamefacedly, "Well, I stopped weighing myself when I reached 180. I knew I'd gained a bit more, but this is unbelievable. Are you sure your scale isn't out of order?" He laughed in embarrassment and went on, "I admit that my heart has been acting a little funny lately, and I became afraid that I might be carrying too much fat. Can you help me?"

After he had a complete physical examination by his physician, whom he had been avoiding, he was referred back to me by his doctor. A serious, intelligent gentleman, Mr. Zimmerman took to touch-control and my diet immediately, and followed the program precisely. After he reached his target weight of 165 pounds, he phoned: "My doctor says that my ticker is OK now and that I'm in better shape than I've been for years."

The significant point for you here is that many people who gain weight in the usual course of living, or regain it after most reducing diets, just block out the reality. They fool themselves, thinking that they are thinner than they really are even as their clothes become too tight and they avoid the truth reflected in the mirror and on the scale. With the revolutionary aid of touch-control and the entire program, you're not likely to let that happen to you—but don't let your guard down ever.

RETURN TO THE DIET IMMEDIATELY

Obviously, it's best if you cut down your eating if you see the numbers on the scale go up two or three pounds more than your target weight. If you get on the scale one morning and see that you've gone five pounds over your cherished number set for trimness, maximum health, and good looks, *go right back on the DeBetz Diet that same day!*

As you learned when you began dieting, use the stop and

support procedures completed with STOPlines and SUPPORTlines repeatedly at once, at least a few times daily, as part of lifetime weight maintenance. You know well all the instructions that worked in reducing you. Put them to full use again now.

It will be much easier for you to succeed on your return to the full reducing program because it worked so well for you when you lost far more than five pounds. First, do this: Set aside a few minutes of private time with yourself in a quiet place where you like to be. In the usual touch-control procedure, touch your face with a finger, look upward, close your eyes, and keep them closed as you say the STOPlines to yourself or aloud, as you please:

> For my body, overeating is an insult
>   and a poison.
> I need my body to live.
> I owe my body this respect and attention.

Relax completely for a moment, finger still touching your face gently, eyes closed, as you think quietly of the words you've just repeated.

Now, keeping your relaxed position, finger still touching your face, eyes closed, repeat the parts of the support procedure where you looked at yourself with your mind's eye, as you did so often during your reducing period.

Take time to scan your slimmed naked body in your mind's mirror. Admire your body inch by inch as trimmed down from its previous overweight—as if you're viewing it on a TV screen inside your head. Take a moment to enjoy feeling pride in yourself and your success in taking off the excess pounds that threatened your health and appearance.

Continue in this period of quiet and peace with yourself to delight in the inner view of the transformation of your overweight body into the trimmer, healthier, more graceful body you now enjoy at rest and in motion. Tell yourself emphatically: "This is the trim body I will maintain always. This is how I'm going to look always. I will never allow myself to be heavy again."

Remove your hand so that your fingertip no longer touches

your face. Then open your eyes and feel thoroughly refreshed, eager to return to the diet plus touch-control boosters for the brief period required. Realize and be reassured by the fact that you need to take off only five pounds now, not the much greater excess weight you had to reduce originally. Furthermore, you've had the successful experience, so you know you'll be back to your target trimness in no time.

If you hit the five-pound warning number, it's also a good idea to reread the early chapters slowly and in full detail, as if for the first time. You'll find that remarkably supportive and helpful again. As I keep saying in respect to the "magic touch" that is your concentration signal, we all need reminders.

YOURS NOW: A WONDERFUL NEW LIFE-STYLE

As you probably are beginning to realize, permanent weight reduction makes certain wonderful changes in your life-style. You definitely form new attitudes toward your body and your health. You will have developed new eating habits, perhaps without realizing it fully as it happens. You commit yourself to daily increased regular activity.

Acquiring these very desirable changes requires effort. They become increasingly natural for you, and eventually become automatic, as automatic as your overeating habits were before. You should feel highly gratified, reassured that having attained your ideal weight, you don't have to keep dieting any more. You're now equipped with healthy new thin eating habits.

This is the secret of enduring trimness: making this way of healthier eating a natural part of you. Inevitably you develop an ingrained preference for the clean, tasty, ungreasy low-caloric servings that helped you reduce. You'll come to like them so well that the preference remains with you forever. So many of my reduced patients have told me, "Ugh, I can't stand overly rich, fatty, high-calorie dishes anymore." It follows automatically that your weight remains controlled readily.

MORE WAYS THAT WORK TO HELP YOU STAY TRIM

Add new dimensions to your life to go along with your new eating attitudes and habits. These, too, help make food and eating of less consequence in your daily living. Arrange and enjoy an active social schedule. Once you're thin and more attractive, you don't feel that you have to hide anymore.

But while you're socializing, never forget your commitment to staying trim. Always follow your own new thin-eating guidelines without regard to the eating activities of others. Remember my assurance that you have the right to say "no" if someone tries to push food on you. Think of this: Small children learn earlier to say "no" than "yes"—see how determinedly a child says "no" if mother tries to push food into her or his mouth. You too can say "no" to anyone forcing food on you.

Plan activities that don't include eating. There are so many enjoyable alternatives. Instead of meeting a friend for a meal, suggest a pleasant brisk walk, capped with a steaming pot of coffee, tea, or espresso (no cream or sugar, of course). Yes, much social life revolves around food, but be creative and minimize the serving of food with social activities. Believe me, most others will join in gratefully and applaud you for your initiative.

Alter your customary daily schedule if you've noticed by analyzing your comings and goings that you habitually crave food at specific times or in certain situations. Rearrange your activities to avoid or change those "danger" times and occurrences. The impulse to eat in those circumstances is often a "conditioned reflex," when you act without thinking.

That reflex will vanish once you change your schedule purposely. For instance, many of my overweight patients told me something like "As soon as I walk into my apartment, I throw off my coat and head for the refrigerator—and before I know it, I'm stuffing food into my mouth." When I instruct them to arrange something else—to get into the habit of showering immediately, washing up and changing clothes, relaxing with a magazine and a sugar-free drink, or whatever foodless activity pleases them—they break the vicious circle.

"And above all," I remind them, "use your touch-control action tool and STOPlines and then your SUPPORTlines procedure to stop you from opening the refrigerator without a thought. Never forget to apply 'the pause that reinforces.' " It works for my formerly overweight patients—it will work for you.

Make eating a specific isolated activity so that when you eat, either with or without others, you choose carefully what and how you eat, and then you chew and sip and savor s-l-o-w-l-y. No stuffing or hurried swallowing or gulping. Make eating a conscious act, never unconscious and unthinking.

By being aware of each bite and sip, you'll appreciate the food more—and consequently eat less. An example of "unconscious eating" was reported by one of my patients, Rosa Gillespie, 23, a store cashier. "I came home so exhausted last night that I just collapsed into an armchair in front of the TV set, turned on a program, and stared at it. My father had left a full can of peanuts on the arm of the chair.

"Fifteen minutes later I turned off the set and got up to take a shower. I stared at the can of peanuts—it was empty. I was in shock—I had eaten them all, about a zillion calories, and I didn't enjoy a single bite because I didn't even know I was eating them!" She sighed. "I didn't think of touch-control because I was so zonked out. I'll never do that again—from now on I'll know what I'm eating." After that crisis, Rosa kept to her vow and lost weight steadily. She's now slim, lovely, and lively.

Note this very important repeat warning: Don't eat without being fully aware of exactly what you're doing and what you're eating. Don't eat at the same time that you're watching TV, reading, listening to the radio or cassettes, talking on the telephone —none of those activities where your mind is fixed primarily on something other than eating. By being totally conscious of your eating, you'll avoid loads of "unconscious" calories.

Avoid rewarding yourself by eating. Instead, choose from any number of available nonfattening rewards. If you feel that you need or want a reward, give yourself something more enduring than food—such as an article of clothing, anywhere from a scarf or necktie to a new dress or suit. Perhaps you'd enjoy a special manicure or facial, a treat that you wouldn't allow yourself ordinarily.

Another possibility: If you have a loving spouse or friend or close family members, invite them to participate in your reward system. One of my patients said that her husband promised to reward her with a new pair of earrings each year if she maintained her trimmed-down weight. She told me delightedly, "The first year he gave me gold hoops, the second year pearls, and now at the end of the third year beautiful diamond studs. And he still doesn't know that with touch-control and your blueprint, I'd stay slim anyhow!" Involving a partner is fun, during and after dieting.

Learn to control your emotions, instead of your emotions controlling you and driving you to overeat. Many overweights blame pressures of negative feelings, like the woman mentioned earlier who attributed her downfall to f-a-t: frustration, anxiety, and tension. Others accuse boredom, and even feeling suddenly excited and happy: "I was so exhilarated by my success that I treated myself to a triple-scoop fudge ice-cream cone topped with candy sprinkles!"

Instead of blaming something bad or good for any overindulgence, sit back and pause for reinforcement through a minute of thought and use of your touch-control tool and STOPlines. There's no question that you'll feel relieved and pleased with yourself for not stuffing your mouth and stomach. Realize that whatever emotional relief you hope to get from an eating reward is short-lived. What's more, you'll be angry with yourself for gorging—another destructive emotion.

Create a personal "paced" eating routine. Teach yourself to pace your eating so that you chew well and enjoy every bite slowly. Put down your fork between bites, and swallow what you have in your mouth before you take the next forkful.

Consider that it takes about 20 minutes for food to be absorbed, and a certain amount of time for your stomach to signal to your brain that you've eaten enough. By slowing down and pacing your eating, you give your body a chance to digest and respond to what you've eaten. The result: You feel fuller with less food.

Avoid situations that you find highly tempting. It's a fact that the sight and smell of food are powerful stimuli to eat. For instance, if you know from past experience that passing a certain aromatic pizzeria makes you want to rush in and buy a pizza, detour beforehand. In short, always be on your toes to avoid temptations that are destructive to your new thin eating habits. You can always stop yourself by using the touch action, but why invite temptation?

At home, make food less visible and accessible than in the past. Keep nuts, candy, cookies, rich snacks in closed containers, out of sight, not out where you might grab and munch without thinking. Since you've worked conscientiously on your attractive new body and new slimming eating habits, keep junk foods out of the refrigerator and cupboard as much as possible. Replace them with tasty, nutritious fruits and delicious low-calorie snacks, such as those listed in chapter 4.

"TO LENGTHEN THY LIFE, LESSEN THY MEALS"

That wise advice was passed on by Benjamin Franklin some 200 years ago, and is valid today as part of your lifelong stay-trim blueprint. To help promote your good health and long life, I recommend that at least for the first few months of starting your maintenance program you reread this chapter several times. And don't forget to refer to other chapters to refresh your accurate knowledge about using touch-control and adhering to the DeBetz Diet.

Also continue to practice touch-control daily for further reinforcement. Be reassured that you are reaching the point where it will all be second nature to you. Take it from me, there's no question about that. I know not only from all my successful trim patients, but from personal experience. Despite being heavy in my earlier years, I have now maintained my ideal weight within a five-pound range for decades by following the recommendations in this book. I usually cut back on my eating if I gain two or three pounds over my ideal weight, rather than waiting until the scale shows five pounds over.

Believe me, I don't feel deprived in the least if I eat a bowl of delicious fresh strawberries instead of a thick slice of chocolate mousse cake. You too can get there, maintain your weight, and stay trim for the rest of your healthier life.

12

DETAILED CONTENTS
CHECKLIST TO AID
CHOICE OF FOODS

Amounts of Calories, Protein,
Fat, Carbohydrates

As you know by now, I provide clear, usable instructions always —to help you take off your excess weight, and keep it off. That's what all my successful formerly overweight patients have accomplished, and so can you. Some of them may have had a good deal more weight to lose than you, yet I know from the many who kept in touch with me that they not only took off the excess pounds, but kept them off year after year.

I have avoided any complicated, impractical information and instructions. For one thing, as I stated from the start, you don't count calories on the DeBetz Diet, even though calories count in regard to putting on or taking off weight. Asking dieters to count the calories in everything they eat at every meal, and all day long for a lifetime, just doesn't work. You've probably heard the quip that "most overweight people who claim they count calories turn out to be poor mathematicians—and they have the figures to prove it."

I include the comprehensive, detailed calories checklist here so you'll have it for handy repeated reference if you wish to consult it at any time. The checklist can be helpful to you particularly as part of your lifetime stay-trim blueprint in selecting lower-calorie foods in a category. By referring to the checklist, as often as you care to, you'll have an idea of calorie trade-offs in the different kinds of foods. You can make a stay-trim choice accordingly when you're shopping, preparing meals, eating at home and at dinner parties and in restaurants.

Here are a few examples of the kind of helpful information you can make part of your knowledge to help stay at your desired weight by referring repeatedly to the checklist. Calorie counts cannot be 100 percent precise but are useful for comparison purposes. Whatever type of food you are considering for a meal, note the basic wide variation in calories within that food group:

Fish: You might select flounder or sole at 79 calories for 3½ ounces uncooked—or bluefish at 117 calories for the same amount. Obviously, eating the sole instead of bluefish would be helpful in keeping your weight down.

Chicken, meats: 3½ ounces, cooked, of chicken without the skin is 166 calories. The same amount of lean steak is 201 calories; lean lamb, 186 calories; lean hamburger, 216 calories; regular market ground hamburger, 286 calories. You can make some surprising savings in calories according to your selections.

Vegetables, 1 cup cooked: green beans, 25 calories; lima beans, 197 calories; red kidney beans, 234 calories; spinach, 45 calories; zucchini, 35 calories; peas, 110 calories. A check will show you that raw vegetables such as carrots, celery, lettuce, peppers, radishes, tomatoes, and watercress are very low in calories.

Fruit: Medium-size peach, 33 calories; 2 peach halves canned in syrup, 96 calories; fresh strawberries, 1 cup, 55 calories; frozen strawberries, sliced, sweetened, 1 cup, 247 calories; grapefruit, half, 50 calories; canned grapefruit, sweetened, 1 cup, 130 calories.

Milk, 1 cup: whole milk, 157 calories; skim milk, 86 calories; 98 percent fat-free milk, 125 calories; lactose-reduced low-fat milk, 100 calories.

Desserts: Gelatin dessert, sugar-free, ½ cup, 8 calories; regular gelatin dessert, ½ cup, 80 calories (ten times as many as sugar-free!).

Soups, canned, 1 cup: Vegetable soup, 80 calories; bean soup, 190 calories; bouillon, consommé, 10 calories.

Please note again that in soups or any foods on the calorie list, the method of preparation and ingredients used in cooking can cause wide variations in total calories. With this in mind, the checklist numbers still provide a valuable basic guide.

For your general knowledge and interests, the checklist also informs you of the amount of protein, fat, and carbohydrates in most of the items. Eating according to the DeBetz Diet daily listings is excellent preparation for selecting foods, and planning and choosing meals, to maintain the healthful nutritional balance of about 33 percent protein, 16 percent fat, and 51 percent complex carbohydrates. Of course, I don't expect you to count the P-F-C in everything you eat each day, in order to arrive at that balance.

So keep referring to the checklist repeatedly or not, as you personally see fit. The data is derived from checking with a variety of sources, including our own research, and from listings in the excellent USDA handbook *Composition of Foods*, produced by the Agricultural Research Service of the United States Department of Agriculture (offered by the Superintendent of Documents, U.S. Government Printing Office, Washington, D.C. 20402).

MEASUREMENTS

By Weight:

1 ounce equals 28.35 grams
100 grams equal 3.57 ounces
16 ounces equal 1 pound

By Volume:

1 cup equals 8 fluid ounces or ½ pint or 16 tablespoons
1 tablespoon equals 3 teaspoons
2 tablespoons equal 1 fluid ounce
1 pint equals 2 cups
1 quart equals 4 cups

FOOD CONTENTS LISTINGS: CALORIES, PROTEIN, FAT, CARBOHYDRATES

Listed in the following order:

- Poultry and meats
- Fish and shellfish
- Vegetables
- Fruits and fruit products
- Milk, cheese, eggs, related foods
- Fats, oils, shortenings
- Grain products: Breads, cereals, cakes, grains
- Sweets, sugar, nuts
- Beverages
- Soups, jams, miscellaneous

FOODS: PORTION	CALORIES	PROTEIN (grams)	FAT (grams)	CARBO-HYDRATES (grams)
POULTRY AND MEATS				
Bacon, crisp, drained, thin-sliced: 2 slices	95	5	8	1
Bacon, Canadian, crisp, drained, trimmed: 1 oz.	79	8	5	trace
Beef, trimmed, cooked:				
Braised, simmered, pot-roasted:				
lean and fat: 3½ oz.	286	27	19	0
lean only: 3½ oz.	196	31	7	0
Hamburger, broiled:				
regular market ground:				
3½ oz.	286	24.5	20	0
ground lean: 3½ oz.	216	27	11.5	0
Rib or other relatively fat roast, oven-cooked without liquid:				
lean and fat: 3½ oz.	455	19	42	0
lean only: 3½ oz.	233	27	14	0
Round or other relatively lean cut:				
lean and fat: 3½ oz.	256	27	16	0
lean only: 3½ oz.	182	29	5.5	0

FOODS: PORTION	CALORIES	PROTEIN (grams)	FAT (grams)	CARBO-HYDRATES (grams)
Steak, broiled: relatively fat, such as sirloin:				
lean and fat: 3½ oz.	385	23	31.5	0
lean only: 3½ oz.	201	31.5	7	0
Porterhouse:				
57% lean, 43% fat:				
3½ oz.	465	19.5	42	0
separable lean: 3½ oz.	224	30	10.5	0
T-bone:				
56% lean, 44% fat:				
3½ oz.	473	19.5	43	0
separable lean: 3½ oz.	223	30	10	0
Club steak:				
58% lean, 42% fat:				
3½ oz.	454	20.5	40.5	0
separable lean: 3½ oz.	244	29.5	13	0
Beef, corned beef:				
cooked, medium fat:				
3½ oz.	372	23	30	0
canned lean: 3½ oz.	185	26	8	0
Beef, dried or chipped: 2 oz.	372	23	30	0
Beef liver, fried: 3½ oz.	229	26	10.5	5.5
cooked without fat (or raw): 3½ oz.	140	20	4	5.5
Beef tongue:				
cooked, braised: 3½ oz.	244	21.5	17	0
canned or pickled: 3½ oz.	267	19	20	trace
Chicken, cooked:				
Broilers:				
flesh and skin, broiled, without bone: 3½ oz.	216	28	11	0
light meat, without skin: 3½ oz.	166	31.5	3.5	0
dark meat, without skin: 3½ oz.	176	28	6	0
Roasters:				
flesh and skin, roasted: 3½ oz.	248	27	14.5	0
flesh only, roasted: 3½ oz.	183	29.5	6	0

FOODS: PORTION	CALORIES	PROTEIN (grams)	FAT (grams)	CARBO-HYDRATES (grams)
canned, boneless:				
3½ oz.	170	25	7	0
Livers, simmered:				
3½ oz.	165	26.5	4.5	3
Duck, domestic, roasted:				
4 oz.	370	18	32	0
Goose, domestic, roasted:				
4 oz.	480	27	42	0
Lamb:				
Leg (choice grade): total edible, cooked, roasted (83% lean, 17% fat):				
3½ oz.	279	25	19	0
separable lean, roasted:				
3½ oz.	186	28.5	7	0
Loin (choice grade): total edible, broiled chops (72% lean, 25% fat):				
3½ oz.	293	16.5	25	0
separable lean, broiled chops: 3½ oz.	188	28	7.5	0
Shoulder (choice grade): cooked, roasted (74% lean, 26% fat): 3½ oz.	338	21.5	27	0
separable lean: 3½ oz.	205	27	10	0
Pork, fresh: composite of trimmed, lean cuts: ham, loin, shoulder, and spareribs:				
medium fat class, cooked, roasted (77% lean, 23% fat): 3½ oz.	373	22.5	30.5	0
separable lean: 3½ oz.	236	28	13	0
Chop, thick, with bone:				
3½ oz.	260	16	21	0
Chop, lean only: 1.7 oz.	130	15	7	0
Roast, oven-cooked, no liquid added:				
lean and fat: 3 oz.	310	21	24	0
lean only: 2.4 oz.	175	20	10	0

FOODS: PORTION	CALORIES	PROTEIN (grams)	FAT (grams)	CARBO-HYDRATES (grams)
Pork, cured:				
Ham, medium-fat: cooked, roasted (84% lean, 16% fat): 3½ oz.	289	21	22	0
separable lean: 3½ oz.	187	25	9	0
canned: 3½ oz.	287	18	12	1
Picnic:				
cooked, roasted (82% lean, 18% fat): 3½ oz.	323	22.5	25	0
separable lean: 3½ oz.	211	28.5	10	0
Rabbit, cooked, stewed: 3½ oz.	216	29	10	0
Sausage, cold cuts, and luncheon meats:				
Bologna (average): 3½ oz.	277	13.5	23	3.5
Braunschweiger: 3½ oz.	319	15	27.5	2.5
Cervelat (soft): 3½ oz.	307	18.5	24.5	1.5
Country-style sausage: 3½ oz.	345	15	31	0
Deviled ham, canned: 3½ oz.	351	14	32.5	0
Frankfurters, cooked: 3½ oz.	304	12.5	27	1.5
Liverwurst, smoked: 3½ oz.	319	15	27.5	2.5
Luncheon meat:				
Boiled ham: 3½ oz.	234	19	17	0
Pork sausage, links or bulk, cooked: 3½ oz.,	476	18	44	trace
Salami, dry: 3½ oz.	450	24	38	1
Sweetbreads:				
Beef, cooked: 3½ oz.	320	26	23	0
Calf, cooked: 3½ oz.	168	32.5	3	0
Lamb, cooked: 3½ oz.	175	28	6	0
Turkey:				
total edible, cooked, roasted: 3½ oz.	263	27	16.5	0
flesh and skin, roasted: 3½ oz.	223	32	9.5	0
flesh only, cooked, roasted: 3½ oz.	190	31.5	6	0

FOODS: PORTION	CALORIES	PROTEIN (grams)	FAT (grams)	CARBO-HYDRATES (grams)
light meat, cooked, roasted: 3½ oz.	176	33	4	0
dark meat, cooked, roasted: 3½ oz.	203	30	8.5	0
Veal:				
average cut, medium fat, trimmed, roasted (86% lean, 14% fat): 3½ oz.	216	28.5	10.5	0
cutlet, broiled without bone: 3 oz.	185	23	9	4
FISH AND SHELLFISH				
Anchovy, canned: 3 fillets	21	2.5	1	trace
Bass, black sea:				
poached, broiled, or baked without fat: 3½ oz.	93	19	1	0
Bass, striped raw: 3½ oz.	105	19	2.5	0
Bluefish, raw: 3½ oz.	117	20.5	3.5	0
Clams, raw, meat only: 3½ oz.	76	12.5	1.5	2
canned, drained: 3½ oz.	98	16	2.5	2
juice: 3½ oz.	19	2.5	trace	2
Cod, cooked or broiled:				
3½ oz.	170	28.5	5.5	0
dried, salted: 3½ oz.	130	29	1	0
Crab, Dungeness, rock, and King, cooked, steamed:				
3½ oz.	93	17.5	2	.5
Fish sticks, frozen, cooked:				
3½ oz.	176	16.5	9	6.5
Flounder, raw: 3½ oz.	79	16.5	1	0
Haddock, raw: 3½ oz.	79	18.5	trace	0
Halibut, Atlantic and Pacific, cooked, broiled: 3½ oz.	171	25	7	0
Herring, raw:				
Atlantic: 3½ oz.	176	17.5	11.5	0
Pacific: 3½ oz.	98	17.5	2.5	0
canned, tomato sauce:				
3½ oz.	176	16	10.5	3.5
pickled: 3½ oz.	223	20.5	15	0
salted or brined: 3½ oz.	218	19	15	0
kippered: 3½ oz.	211	22	13	0

FOODS: PORTION	CALORIES	PROTEIN (grams)	FAT (grams)	CARBO-HYDRATES (grams)
Lobster, northern, canned or cooked: 3½ oz.	95	19	1.5	.5
Mackerel, canned: 3½ oz.	183	19.5	11	0
salted: 3½ oz.	305	18.5	25	0
smoked: 3½ oz.	219	24	13	0
Mussels, meat only: 3½ oz.	95	14.5	2	3.5
Ocean perch (redfish): 3½ oz.	88	18	1	0
Octopus, raw: 3½ oz.	73	15.5	1	0
Oysters, raw: Eastern: 3½ oz.	66	8.5	2	3.5
Western: 3½ oz.	91	10.5	2	6.5
Oysters, fried: 3½ oz.	239	8.5	14	18.5
Pike, broiled: 3½ oz.	90	19	1	0
Pompano, raw: 3½ oz.	166	19	9.5	0
Red snapper (and gray), raw: 3½ oz.	93	20	1	0
Salmon, Atlantic, raw: 3½ oz.	217	22.5	13.5	0
canned, solids and liquids: 3½ oz.	203	21.5	12	0
Chinook (King), raw: 3½ oz.	222	19	15.5	0
canned, solids and liquids: 3½ oz.	210	19.5	14	0
Coho, canned, solids and liquids: 3½ oz.	153	21	7	0
cooked, broiled, or baked: 3½ oz.	182	27	7.5	0
smoked: 3½ oz.	176	21.5	9.5	0
Sardines, drained solids: 3¾ oz.	190	18	12.5	1.5
Scallops, bay and sea: cooked, steamed: 3½ oz.	112	23	1.5	1
frozen, breaded, fried, reheated: 3½ oz.	194	18	8.5	10.5
Sea bass, white, raw: 3½ oz.	96	21.5	.5	0
Shad, raw: 3½ oz.	170	18.5	10	0
Shrimp, canned, meat only: 3½ oz.	116	24	1	1
French fried: 3½ oz.	225	20.5	11	10

FOODS: PORTION	CALORIES	PROTEIN (grams)	FAT (grams)	CARBO-HYDRATES (grams)
Smelts, 4–5, raw:	100	19	2	0
Sole, raw (also flounder, sand crabs): 3½ oz.	79	16.5	1	0
Swordfish, raw: 3½ oz.	118	19	4	0
Trout, brook, raw: 3½ oz.	101	19	2	0
rainbow or steelhead, raw: 3½ oz.	195	21.5	11.5	0
Tuna, canned in oil:				
solids and liquid: 3½ oz.	288	24	20.5	0
drained solids: 3½ oz.	197	29	8	0
canned in water: 3½ oz.	127	28	1	0
Weakfish, raw: 3½ oz.	121	16.5	5.5	0
Whitefish, lake, raw: 3½ oz.	155	19	8	0
smoked: 3½ oz.	155	20	7.5	0
VEGETABLES				
Artichoke, cooked: 3½ oz.	44	3	trace	10
Artichoke hearts, frozen: 3 oz.	22	1	trace	4
Asparagus, med. spear, canned:	3	trace	trace	.5
6 spears	20	2	trace	3
Avocado, large: ½	180	2	16.5	6
Bamboo shoots, raw: 3½ oz.	27	2.5	trace	5
Bean sprouts:				
cooked (mung beans): 1 cup	28	3	trace	5
raw: 1 cup	26	3	trace	4
Bean sprouts (soybean): 1 cup	50	7	1	5
Beans, green, cooked: 1 cup	25	2	trace	6
wax, cooked: 1 cup	22	1.5	trace	4.5
lima (green), cooked: 1 cup	197	13	1	35
dry lima, cooked: 1 cup	265	15.5	1	49
red kidney, cooked: 1 cup	234	15	1	42.5
Beets, diced: 1 cup	70	2	trace	16
Broccoli: 1 cup	50	5	trace	8
Brussels sprouts, cooked: 1 cup	50	5.5	.5	8.5

FOODS: PORTION	CALORIES	PROTEIN (grams)	FAT (grams)	CARBO-HYDRATES (grams)
Cabbage, raw, shredded:				
1 cup	25	1	trace	5
cooked: 1 cup	40	2	trace	9
Cabbage (Chinese cabbage):				
raw 1″ pieces: 1 cup	15	1	trace	2
cooked: 1 cup	25	2	1	4
Carrots, 5½″, raw: 1 cup	20	1	trace	5
diced: 1 cup	45	1	1	9
Cauliflower, cooked, florets:				
1 cup	30	3	trace	6
Celery, 8″ stalk, raw:	5	1	trace	1
diced, cooked: 1 cup	20	1	trace	4
Chard, Swiss, cooked: 1 cup	30	2.7	.3	5
Chick-peas, dry, raw: ½ cup	360	20	4.5	60
Chives, chopped, fresh: 1 tbs.	3	.2	0	.5
Collards, leaves, cooked:				
1 cup	65	7	1.3	10
Corn, cooked, 5″ ear	65	2	1	16
canned, with liquid: 1 cup	170	5	1	41
Cucumber, 1 med. raw:	16	1	trace	3
6⅛″ center slices	5	trace	trace	1
pickle, sweet, 1 med.	146	.5	trace	36.5
pickle, sour or dill: 1 large	11	.5	trace	22
Eggplant, cooked: 1 cup	34	2	trace	7
Endive, fresh: 1 cup	10	1	trace	2
(escarole, chicory) Belgian				
endive, 4″: 1	5	trace	trace	1
Kale, cooked: 1 cup	45	4	1	8
Kohlrabi, cooked: 1 cup	36	2.5	trace	8
Leeks, raw: 1 cup	104	4	.5	22
Lentils, cooked: 1 cup	212	15.5	trace	39.5
Lettuce, head, fresh: loose				
leaf, 4″ diam.: 1 head	30	3	trace	6
compact, 4¾″ diam.:				
1 head	70	4	.5	12.5
2 large or 4 small leaves	5	1	trace	trace
Mushrooms, cooked or				
canned: 1 cup	41	4.5	trace	5.5
Okra, cooked: 8 pods	30	2	trace	6

FOODS: PORTION	CALORIES	PROTEIN (grams)	FAT (grams)	CARBO-HYDRATES (grams)
Olives,				
green: 1 large	9	trace	1	trace
ripe: 1 large	13	trace	1.5	trace
Onions, mature: raw, 2½"				
diam.: 1 onion	50	2	trace	11
cooked: 1 cup	80	2	trace	18
Onions, young green, small,				
no tops: 6 onions	25	trace	trace	5
Parsley, fresh, chopped: 1 tbs.	1	trace	trace	trace
Parsnips, cooked: 1 cup	95	2	1	22
Peas, green: cooked, 1 cup	110	8	1	19
canned, with liquid: 1 cup	170	8	1	32
Peppers,				
sweet, green: 1 medium	15	1	trace	3
red: 1 pod	20	1	trace	3
Potatoes, med. (about 3 lbs.):				
baked, after peeling:				
1 potato	90	3	trace	21
boiled, peeled after				
boiling: 1 potato	105	3	trace	23
boiled, peeled before				
boiling: 1 potato	90	3	trace	21
French fried, 1 piece 2" x				
½" x ½": 10 pieces	155	2	7	20
chips, medium, 2" diam.:				
10 chips	110	1	7	10
mashed (with milk added):				
1 cup	145	4	1	30
Pumpkin, canned: 1 cup	83	2	1	18
Radishes, small: 4	10	trace	trace	2
Rutabagas, cooked, diced:				
1 cup	70	1.8	.2	16
Sauerkraut, canned, drained:				
1 cup	30	2	trace	6
Soybeans, mature, cooked:				
1 cup	277	22	11.5	21.5
immature, raw	284	22	10	26
Spinach, cooked: 1 cup	45	6	1	6
Squash, cooked:				
summer, diced: 1 cup	35	1	trace	8

FOODS: PORTION	CALORIES	PROTEIN (grams)	FAT (grams)	CARBO-HYDRATES (grams)
winter, baked, mashed:				
1 cup	126	3	.5	30
summer, raw: 1 cup	38	2	trace	8
Sweet potatoes:				
baked (1 sweet potato 5″ x 2″)	155	2	1	36
boiled (1 sweet potato 5″ x 2″)	170	2	1	39
candied (1 sweet potato 3½″ x 2¼″)	295	2	6	60
Tomatoes:				
fresh, 1 medium 2″ x 2½″	30	2	trace	6
canned, or cooked: 1 cup	45	2	trace	9
Tomato juice, canned: 1 cup	50	2	trace	9
Tomato ketchup: 1 tbs.	15	trace	trace	4
Turnips, cooked, diced:				
1 cup	40	1	trace	9
Vegetable juice, cocktail,				
canned or bottled: 6 oz.	31	1.5	trace	6.5
Water chestnuts, Chinese,				
fresh: 4 average	20	trace	trace	4.5
Watercress: 1 cup	10	1	trace	1.5
Zucchini	35	1	trace	8

FRUITS AND FRUIT PRODUCTS

FOODS: PORTION	CALORIES	PROTEIN (grams)	FAT (grams)	CARBO-HYDRATES (grams)
Apples, fresh: 1 medium (2½″ diam.)	70	trace	trace	18
Applesauce, fresh: 1 cup	125	trace	0	32
Applesauce, canned:				
sweetened: 1 cup	185	trace	trace	47
unsweetened: 1 cup	100	trace	trace	25
Apple juice, cider: 4 oz.	52	trace	0	12.5
Apricots, fresh, 12 per lb.: 3	60	1	trace	14
canned in heavy syrup:				
1 cup	218	1.5	trace	53
dried, uncooked, 40				
halves, small: 1 cup	390	7.5	1	89
cooked, unsweetened,				
fruit and liquid: 1 cup	260	5	1	62
nectar: 1 cup	143	1	trace	34

FOODS: PORTION	CALORIES	PROTEIN (grams)	FAT (grams)	CARBO-HYDRATES (grams)
Banana, fresh, about 3 per lb.: 1	130	2	trace	30.5
Blackberries, fresh: 1 cup	85	2	1	17
Blueberries, fresh: 1 cup	89	1	1	19
Cantaloupe, fresh: ½ melon, 5″ diam.	40	1	trace	9
Cherries:				
fresh, sour: 1 cup	116	2	.5	25
fresh, sweet: 1 cup	140	2.5	.5	32
Cranberries:				
canned sauce, sweetened, strained: 1 cup	400	trace	.5	99
Juice, cocktail, canned: 1 cup	130	trace	trace	32
Cranberry-orange relish, fresh: 3½ oz.	178	trace	trace	45
Dates, dried, pitted:				
1 medium	27	trace	trace	6.5
1 cup	525	4	1	120
Elderberries, fresh: ½ cup	70	2.5	trace	16
Figs, dried, 2″ x 1″: 1 fig	60	1	trace	15
Fruit cocktail, canned, in heavy syrup (with liquid): 1 cup	195	1	trace	47
Gooseberries, fresh: ½ cup	88	1.8	.5	20
Grapefruit, fresh, med., 4½″ diam.: ½ fruit	50	1	trace	12
fresh sections: 1 cup	75	1	trace	18
canned, water pack: 1 cup	70	1	trace	17
juice, fresh: 1 cup	95	1	trace	23
canned:				
unsweetened: 1 cup	100	1	trace	24
sweeteend: 1 cup	130	1	trace	32
frozen concentrate, water added: 1 cup	115	1	trace	28
Grapes, fresh, green:				
seedless, 1 cup	102	1	trace	27
other (approx.): 1 cup	100	1	trace	26
Grape juice, bottled: 1 cup	165	1	trace	42

FOODS: PORTION	CALORIES	PROTEIN (grams)	FAT (grams)	CARBO-HYDRATES (grams)
Lemons, fresh, 2⅓" diam.:				
1 lemon	20	1	trace	6
juice: 1 tbs.	5	trace	trace	1
Lemonade concentrate,				
water added: 1 cup	110	trace	trace	28
Lime juice, fresh: 1 tbs.	4	trace	trace	1
Limeade concentrate, water				
added: 1 cup	103	trace	trace	26
Mandarin oranges, canned				
with syrup: 1 cup	125	1	.5	30
Mango, fresh, edible parts:				
½ lb.	155	1.5	1	35
dried or sliced:				
½ cup: 2½ oz.	53	.5	.3	12
Nectarine, fresh: 1 med.	50	.5	trace	12
Orange, fresh:				
navel, California, 2⅘"				
diam: 1 orange	60	2	trace	13
others, 3" diam.: 1 orange	70	1	trace	17
Orange juice, fresh:				
California: 1 cup	120	2	1	26
Florida: 1 cup	100	1	trace	23
canned, unsweetened:				
1 cup	120	2	trace	28
frozen concentrate, water				
added: 1 cup	110	2	trace	26
Papaya, fresh, ½" cubes: 1 cup	71	1	trace	17
1 large	156	2	trace	38
Peaches, fresh, medium:				
2" diam. (4 per lb): 1 peach	33	.5	trace	8
sliced: 1 cup	65	1	trace	16
canned, heavy syrup: 2				
halves, 2 tbs. syrup	96	trace	trace	24
water pack: 1 cup	75	1	trace	19
Peach nectar, canned: 1 cup	124	trace	trace	31
Pears, fresh (3" x 2½" diam.):				
1 pear	100	1	1	24
canned in heavy syrup,				
halves or slices: 1 cup	200	1	trace	50
canned, water packed:				
1 cup	80	trace	trace	20

FOODS: PORTION	CALORIES	PROTEIN (grams)	FAT (grams)	CARBO-HYDRATES (grams)
Pear nectar, canned: 1 cup	130	1	trace	33
Persimmons, Japanese or				
Kaki, fresh, 2½″ diam.: 1	80	1	trace	20
Pineapple				
fresh, diced: 1 cup	75	1	trace	19
canned in syrup, crushed:				
1 cup	205	1	trace	50
sliced (slices and juice):				
2 sm.	95	trace	trace	25
canned, packed in own				
syrup: 3½ oz.	58	trace	trace	15
Pineapple juice, canned:				
1 cup	120	1	trace	31
Plums (not prunes):				
fresh, 2″ diam., about 2 oz.:				
1 plum	30	trace	trace	7
canned in syrup: 3 plums,				
2 tbs. juice	90	trace	trace	23
Prunes, dried:				
medium, 50 or 60 per lb: 4	80	1	trace	19
cooked, unsweetened,				
17–18 prunes and ⅓ cup				
liquid: 1 cup	330	3	1	80
Prune juice, canned: 1 cup	185	1	trace	42
Raisins, dried: 1 cup	462	4	trace	111
Raspberries, red, fresh: 1 cup	70	1	.5	16
frozen, sweetened: 1 cup	196	1.5	trace	47
Rhubarb, cooked, sugar				
added: 1 cup	385	1	trace	98
Strawberries, fresh: 1 cup	55	1	1	11
frozen, sliced, sweetened:				
1 cup	247	1	trace	60
Tangerines, fresh 2½″ diam.,				
about 4 per lb.: 1	40	1	trace	10
Tangerine juice, canned:				
unsweetened: 1 cup	105	1	trace	25
frozen, water added: 1 cup	115	1	trace	27
Watermelon, fresh: 4″ x 8″				
wedge	240	4.5	2	52
balls or cubes: 1 cup	56	1	trace	12

FOODS: PORTION	CALORIES	PROTEIN (grams)	FAT (grams)	CARBO-HYDRATES (grams)
MILK, CHEESE, EGGS, RELATED FOODS				
Cheese (1 ounce except				
where otherwise noted)				
American	106	6	9	.5
American pimiento	106	6	9	.5
Blue	100	6	8	.5
Brie	95	6	8	trace
Camembert	85	6	7	trace
Cheddar	114	7	9.5	.5
Cottage, creamed: ½ cup	117	14	5	3.5
uncreamed: ½ cup	96	19.5	.5	2
pot cheese, low-fat,				
2% fat: ½ cup	101	15.5	2	4
pot cheese, low-fat,				
1% fat: ½ cup	82	14	1	3
Cream	99	2	10	1
Edam	101	7	8	.5
Feta	75	4	6	1
Fontina	110	7	9	.5
Gouda	101	7	8	.5
Limburger	93	6	8	trace
Monterey	106	7	8.5	trace
Mozzarella	80	5.5	6	.5
Mozzarella, part skim	72	7	4.5	1
Muenster	104	6.5	8.5	.5
Neufchâtel	74	3	6.5	1
Parmesan, grated:	111	10	7.5	1
1 tbs.	23	2	1.5	trace
Port du Salut	100	6.5	8	trace
Ricotta: ½ cup	216	14	16	4
Ricotta, part skim: ½ cup	171	14	10	6.5
Romano	110	9	7.5	1
Roquefort	105	6	8.5	.5
Swiss:				
natural, domestic	107	8	7.5	4
processed	95	7	7	.5
Cheese food, American	94	5.5	7	2.5
Cheese spread, American	82	4.5	6	2.5
Cream: 1 tbs.				
half and half	20	.5	1.5	.5

FOODS: PORTION	CALORIES	PROTEIN (grams)	FAT (grams)	CARBO-HYDRATES (grams)
light, table, or coffee	29	.5	3	.5
medium (25% fat)	37	.5	4	.5
sour	26	.5	2.5	.5
sour, imitation, cultured	20	.5	2	.5
whipping cream topping	8	trace	1	.5
whipping, heavy, whipped	26	trace	3	trace
whipping, heavy, unwhipped	52	.5	5.5	.5
whipping, light, whipped	22	trace	2.5	trace
whipping, light, unwhipped	44	.5	4.5	.5
Creamer:				
liquid, frozen: ½ oz.	20	trace	2	1.5
nondairy, powder: 1 tsp.	11	trace	1	1
Milk, canned, undiluted:				
1 fl. oz. condensed, sweetened	123	3	3.5	21
evaporated, whole, un-sweetened: 1 fl. oz.	42	2	2.5	3
evaporated, skim, canned: 1 fl. oz.	25	2.5	trace	3.5
milk, dry, skim:				
nonfat solids: ¼ cup	109	11	trace	15.5
whole	159	8.5	8.5	12.5
fresh (1 cup): 8 fl. oz.: but-termilk, cultured, skim	99	8	2	12
lactose-reduced, low-fat	100	8	2	11
skim	86	8.5	.5	12
skimmed partially, 1% fat	102	8	2.5	11.5
skimmed partially, 2% fat	125	8.5	4.5	12
whole, 3.7% fat	157	8	.9	11.5
Yogurt, plain, low-fat: 1 cup	120	8	4	13
whole-milk: 1 cup	139	8	7.5	10.5
Eggs, chicken, raw or cooked without fat				
white only from 1 large egg	16	3.5	trace	.5
whole, 1 large	79	6	5.5	.5
yolk only from 1 large egg	63	3	5.5	trace
Eggs, dried, whole: 2 tbs.	60	4.5	4	.5

FOODS: PORTION	CALORIES	PROTEIN (grams)	FAT (grams)	CARBO-HYDRATES (grams)
FATS, OILS, SHORTENINGS				
Butter, 4 sticks per lb.				
2 sticks = 1 cup	1,626	2	184	trace
⅛ stick = 1 tbs.	100	trace	11	trace
1 pat (90 per lb.)	36	trace	4	trace
Fats, cooking:				
bacon fat, chicken fat:				
1 tbs.	126	0	14	0
lard: 1 cup	1,985	1	220	0
1 tbs.	124	0	14	0
margarine, 4 sticks per lb.				
2 sticks = 1 cup	1,633	1.5	183	1
⅛ stick = 1 tbs.	102	trace	11	trace
1 pat (80 per lb.)	36	trace	4	trace
Oils, salad or cooking: corn, cottonseed, olive, soy-bean, peanut, safflower oils: 1 tbs.	125	0	14	0
Salad dressings:				
blue cheese: 1 tbs.	90	1	10	.5
imitation-mayonnaise type: 1 tbs.	60	trace	6	2
French: 1 tbs.	60	trace	6	2
mayonnaise: 1 tbs.	110	trace	12	trace
Thousand Island: 1 tbs.	75	trace	8	1
GRAIN PRODUCTS: BREADS, CEREALS, CAKES, GRAINS				
Barley, pearled, uncooked: 1 cup	782	18	2	173
Biscuits, baking powder 2½″ diam.: 1 biscuit	138	3	6.5	17
Bran flakes (40% bran): 1 oz.	87	3	.5	18
Breads:				
cracked wheat (20 slices per lb.): 1 slice	60	2	1	12
French, enriched: 1 slice	58	2	1	11
Italian, enriched: 1 slice	55	2	.5	11
protein: 1 slice	45	2.5	0	8.5
pumpernickel, dark: 1 slice	56	2	trace	12
raisin (20 per loaf): 1 slice	60	2	1	12

FOODS: PORTION	CALORIES	PROTEIN (grams)	FAT (grams)	CARBO-HYDRATES (grams)
rye, light: 1 slice	55	2	trace	12
white, enriched (20 per lb.): 1 slice	60	2	1	12
(26 per lb.): 1 slice	45	1	1	9
whole wheat, graham all-wheat bread (20 per lb.): 1 slice	55	2	1	11
Bread crumbs, dry, grated: 1 cup	345	11	4	65
Cakes:				
angel food cake: 2″ sector of 8″ cake	110	3	trace	23
chocolate, fudge: 2″ sector of 10″ cake	420	5	14	70
fruitcake, dark 2″ x 2″ x ½″: 1 piece	105	2	4	17
gingerbread, 2″ x 2″ x 2″: 1 piece	180	2	7	28
cupcake, plain, 2¾″ diam.: 1 cake	160	3	3	31
pound cake, 2¾″ x 3″ x ⅝″: slice	130	2	7	16
sponge, 2″ sector, 8″ diam. cake: 1 sector	115	3	2	22
Cookies:				
plain and assorted 3″ diam.: 1 cookie	110	2	3	19
fig bars, small: 1	55	1	1	12
Corn flakes, enriched: 1 cup	93	2	trace	21
plain: 1 oz.	110	2	trace	24
presweetened: 1 oz.	115	1	trace	26
Cornmeal, white or yellow, dry: 1 cup	420	11	5	87
Corn muffins, 2¾″ diameter: 1	155	4	5	22
Corn, puffed, presweetened, enriched: 1 oz.	100	1	trace	26
Crackers:				
graham: 4 small or 2 medium	55	1	1	10

FOODS: PORTION	CALORIES	PROTEIN (grams)	FAT (grams)	CARBO-HYDRATES (grams)
saltines, 2″ square:				
2 crackers	35	1	1	6
soda, plain, 2½″ square:				
2 crackers	45	1	1	8
Cracker meal: 1 tbs.	45	1	1	7
Doughnuts, cake type: 1	135	2	7	17
Farina, enriched, cooked:				
1 cup	105	3	trace	22
Macaroni, cooked until				
tender: 1 cup	155	5	1	32
Melba toast: 1 slice	15	.5	trace	2.5
Muffin, with enriched white				
flour: 2¾″ diam.	135	4	5	19
Noodles (egg) cooked,				
enriched: 1 cup	200	7	2	37
Oatmeal or rolled oats,				
cooked: 1 cup	150	5	3	26
Pancakes, 4″ diam.: 1 cake	60	2	2	8
buckwheat: 1 cake	45	2	2	6
Piecrust, enriched, 9″ crust:				
1 crust	655	10	36	72
Pie, 4″ sector of 9″ diam.:				
apple; cherry: 1 sector	330	3	13	53
custard: 1 sector	265	7	11	34
lemon meringue: 1 sector	300	4	12	45
mince: 1 sector	340	3	9	62
pumpkin: 1 sector	265	5	12	34
Pizza (cheese), 5½″ sector, ⅛				
of 14″ pie: 1 sector	180	8	6	23
Popcorn, popped: 1 cup	55	2	1	11
Rice, cooked:				
parboiled: 1 cup	205	4	trace	45
white: 1 cup	200	4	trace	44
Rice, puffed, enriched: 1 cup	55	1	trace	12
Rice flakes, enriched: 1 cup	115	2	trace	26
Rolls, 12 per pound: 1 roll	115	3	2	20
hard, round, 2 oz. ea.:				
1 roll	160	5	2	31
Rye wafers, 1⅞″ x 3½″:				
2 wafers	45	2	trace	10

FOODS: PORTION	CALORIES	PROTEIN (grams)	FAT (grams)	CARBO-HYDRATES (grams)
Spaghetti, cooked until tender: 1 cup	155	5	1	32
Wheat, puffed, enriched:				
1 oz.	100	4	trace	22
presweetened: 1 oz.	105	1	trace	26
Wheat, shredded, plain: 1 oz.	100	4	.5	21
Wheat flakes: 1 oz.	100	3	trace	23
Wheat flours:				
whole wheat: 1 cup	420	16	2	85
all-purpose sifted: 1 cup	400	12	1	84
self-rising: 1 cup	385	10	1	81
Wheat germ: 1 tbs.	24	12	.5	2.5
SWEETS, SUGAR, NUTS				
Almonds, shelled: 1 cup	900	26	77	28
Brazil nuts, broken pieces:				
1 cup	970	20	92	15
Candy:				
caramels: 1 oz.	120	1	3	22
chocolate, sweetened, milk: 1 oz.	151	2	9	16
fudge, plain: 1 oz.	115	trace	3	23
hard candy: 1 oz.	110	0	0	28
marshmallow: 1 oz.	95	1	0	23
Cashew nuts, roasted: 1 cup	570	15	45	26
Coconut, dried, shredded, sweetened: 1 oz.	156	1	11	15
Gelatin, dry, plain: 1 tbs.	35	9	trace	0
Gelatin dessert, prepared:				
plain: 1 cup	155	4	trace	36
with fruit: 1 cup	180	3	trace	42
sugar-free: ½ cup	8	1	0	0
Ice Cream, reg., ½ cup	130	3	7	13.9
Ice milk, ½ cup	100	3	3.5	14.7
Peanuts, roasted, shelled:				
halves: 1 cup	885	37	69	29
chopped: 1 tbs.	52	2	4	2
Peanut butter: 1 tbs.	93	4	8	3
Pecans:				
halves: 1 cup	760	10	74	15

FOODS: PORTION	CALORIES	PROTEIN (grams)	FAT (grams)	CARBO-HYDRATES (grams)
chopped: 1 tbs.	50	1	5	1
Pudding, sugar-free, ½ cup	100	5	3	14
Tofu frozen dessert, ½ cup	210	3.7	7	21
Sherbet: 1 cup	235	3	trace	58
Sugar: 1 oz.	110	0	0	28
Walnuts, chopped: 1 cup	790	17	73	18
1 tbs.	50	1	4.5	1

BEVERAGES
Alcoholic:
Beer, canned or bottled:

	CALORIES	PROTEIN (grams)	FAT (grams)	CARBO-HYDRATES (grams)
regular: 12 fl. oz.	150	1	0	12.5
low-calorie: 12 fl oz.	under 100	1	0	3

Distilled liquor: unflavored
bourbon, brandy,
Canadian whiskey, gin,
Irish whiskey, Scotch
whisky, rum, rye whiskey,

	CALORIES	PROTEIN (grams)	FAT (grams)	CARBO-HYDRATES (grams)
tequila, vodka: 1 fl oz.	65–82*	0	0	trace

Wines:

	CALORIES	PROTEIN (grams)	FAT (grams)	CARBO-HYDRATES (grams)
Champagne, dry brut: 3 oz.	75	trace	0	3.5
dessert (18.8% alcohol): 3 oz.	117	trace	0	6.5
dry (12.2% alcohol): 3 oz.	75	trace	0	3.5

Carbonated (nonalcoholic):
sweetened (quinine

	CALORIES	PROTEIN (grams)	FAT (grams)	CARBO-HYDRATES (grams)
sodas): 8 oz.	71	0	0	18
unsweetened (club soda)	0	0	0	0
cola type: 8 oz.	89	0	0	23
flavored sodas:				
sweetened: 8 oz.	105	0	0	27
unsweetened (diet soda): 8 oz.	—	—	—	—
ginger ale, pale dry and golden: 8 oz.	71	—	—	18
root beer: 8 oz.	94	—	—	24

* Calories average 70 for 86 proof; may vary up or down as indicated if higher or lower proof.

FOODS: PORTION	CALORIES	PROTEIN (grams)	FAT (grams)	CARBO-HYDRATES (grams)
Coffee: 1 cup	2	trace	trace	.5
Tea: 1 cup	2	trace	trace	.5
SOUPS, JAMS, MISCELLANEOUS				
Bouillon cube, ⅝": 1	5	2	trace	trace
Bouillon mix, for 1 cup	10	2	trace	trace
Chili sauce (mostly tomatoes): 1 tbs.	15	trace	trace	4
Chocolate: bitter or unsweetened: 1 oz.	144	3	17.5	8
sweetened: 1 oz.	151	1	10	16.5
Chocolate syrup: 1 tbs.	40	trace	trace	11
Hollandaise sauce: 1 tbs.	48	1	4	2
Honey, strained or extracted: 1 tbs.	64	trace	0	17
Jams, marmalades, preserves: 1 tbs.	55	trace	trace	14
Jellies: 1 tbs.	50	0	0	13
Ketchup, tomato: 1 tbs.	19	trace	trace	4.5
Soups, canned, ready to serve: bean: 1 cup	190	8	5	30
beef: 1 cup	100	6	4	11
bouillon, broth, consommé: 1 cup	10	2	—	0
clam chowder: 1 cup	85	5	2	12
cream soup (asparagus, celery, mushroom): 1 cup	200	7	12	18
noodle, rice, barley: 1 cup	115	6	4	13
pea: 1 cup	140	6	2	25
tomato (with water): 1 cup	86	2	2	15
vegetable: 1 cup	80	5	2	10
Syrup, table blends: 1 tbs.	55	0	0	15
Sugar, granulated, cane, or beet: 1 cup	770	0	0	199
1 tbs.	48	0	0	12

FOODS: PORTION	CALORIES	PROTEIN (grams)	FAT (grams)	CARBO-HYDRATES (grams)
lump, 1⅛″ x ⅝″ x ⅛″:				
1 lump	25	0	0	7
powdered (stirred up):				
1 cup	495	0	0	127
brown, firm-packed: 1 cup	820	0	0	210
1 tbs.	51	0	0	13
Tofu, soft, 1 oz.	22	2.5	trace	1
Vinegar: 1 tbs.	2	0	0	1
White sauce, medium: 1 cup	430	10	33	23

13

WEIGHT-CONTROL ANSWERS THAT WORK

Detailed Answers to Patients' Most-Asked Questions

From the many personal questions about overweight and dieting directed to me by patients during my years of medical practice, here are basic, brief answers to those probably asked most often. While most of the questions have been covered in one way or another earlier in the book, this information can be of further help to you in reaching your desired weight and maintaining it.

Must I Reduce?

Q. I'm 37 years old, and about 30 pounds overweight according to average-weight charts. I'm happily married. My husband doesn't object to my being fat. I feel good in general, just ills most people have. Basically I'm not upset about being a "big" woman. Should I stay as I am or reduce, which I really don't want to do?

A. In spite of the fact that you're content with your body and that your husband doesn't mind, I strongly urge you to lose a large portion of your overweight for medical reasons. It is now well established that overweight has many adverse effects on physical health. This is particularly true if the overweight consists mostly of fat, rather than muscle, which is the case in almost everyone except the highly trained athlete.

If appearance and personal regard are not vital reasons for you to lose weight, matters of health should be. I recommend that you check this book and other authoritative medical sources about the most common chronic diseases associated with excessive weight. The evidence is overwhelming that 30 excess pounds may well bring on minor and serious ills that you and your husband would prefer to avoid.

Does "Born Fat" Mean Fat Lifelong?

Q. I've failed on many diets, and my mother says it's because I'm "naturally fat" or was "born fat." Since I'm over 20, will your diet program reduce me in spite of that?

A. If you've always been overweight, and if you come from a family with a strong history of overweight, odds are that you may have an inborn tendency to gain weight easily. There is a premise called the "fat-cell theory," which infers that some people from infancy have a larger amount of fat cells than others. The person with the increased number of fat cells might gain weight more readily, and experience greater difficulty in keeping his or her weight down.

If you fall into this category, you should accept this as a fact of your life *that you can overcome*. Do everything possible to get your weight down, and then be very strict with yourself to remain within the five-pound limit. If you really have an inborn tendency to be overweight, you can make your desired weight goal a little higher than that in the weight chart. Set a number for yourself that you can reach comfortably and be content with. Losing weight is definitely possible for you, but you must always be alert and not allow yourself to deviate from your commitment. Touch-control plus my diet plan is the different, dependable way for you to reach and maintain your goal.

Feel confident that you can lose weight and stay trim lifelong regardless of any fat-cell theory. Consider it for yourself. How many families do you know with very overweight parents where some offspring are slim? Plenty.

In my medical practice I've had many patients who had heavy parents and despaired of ever being slim. They had failed on other diets. I taught them my two-way system, and they finally lost weight steadily and reported back that they were still trim years later. There's no question in my mind that you can do the same. Go to it.

How to Resist Pressure to "Eat, Eat, Eat"?

Q. I've slimmed down wonderfully with your diet program, but well-meaning relatives and friends keep nagging me that I should eat more because I look too thin, although I think I look great. That "eat, eat, eat" is getting to me. How can I handle it?

A. Learn to assert your right to say "no," as stressed repeatedly in this book. Eating is your private business, and no one has the right to push you to eat more than you want. If your well-meaning relatives and friends don't stop, sit down with them and explain to them that you don't refuse their food because you don't like it, but that you have committed yourself to a way of eating that is important to you.

Also, consider that sometimes relatives equate food and feeding with showing their love to you. If that is so, explain to them that you love them but that food does not have the same meaning to you as it has to them. For you, food is nutrition, not love.

If they still continue and don't take your comments seriously, you may have to resort to some white lies such as pretending that you are allergic to sweets, or that your doctor told you to avoid fried food because of a stomach condition. I prefer open communication, but if this does not work try the second approach. Or tell them frankly that you will avoid seeing them unless they stop nagging you about food and eating.

All You Lose Is Water?

Q. Some people, usually fat, claim that there's no point to dieting, since "all you lose is water." Is that true?

A. Of course not. Don't let anyone get away with telling you that you lose only water when you take off five or ten or many more pounds, and don't regain them. You don't have to be a scientist to recognize the truth of this: When you lose weight, you lose fat and water. If you regain weight, you regain fat and water. When you take off weight and don't regain it, you don't regain either the fat or the water.

So take off your excess weight and keep it off, and don't be concerned about whether you've technically taken off fat or water. Just be delighted that you're slimmer, more vigorous, healthier, and more free-moving and attractive.

Must Skin Sag After Reducing?

Q. I need to lose between 20 and 30 pounds of overweight, but I'm afraid that the skin on my face and body will sag badly. Is there any way I can avoid that?

A. Put your fears away. There are plenty of things that can be done to avoid sagging of the skin. Keep in mind that once you have lost 20 or 30 pounds, you will look younger. Overweight invariably makes people look older; don't forget that the extra pounds are distributed all over, distorting the shape of your body, not just your face and cheeks.

Realize that it is also true that after a certain age the skin has lost some of its elasticity and cannot bounce back as readily as when you were a child or a teenager. But you can counteract that. Here are some of the things you can do if you feel that your skin is sagging:

1. Exercise on a regular basis so that your muscles firm up and fill out any hanging skin.

2. Keep your skin well hydrated. This is very important, although many people don't realize it. If you don't drink enough water, your skin tends to look limp, tired, and saggy. Well-hydrated skin is likely to look fresh, glowing, and crisp. You can observe this with flowers or plants. If you don't water a plant for a couple of days or a week, the leaves will shrivel, droop, and hang, but it perks right up when saturated with water. The same happens with your skin.

As a last resort, if you have lost weight mainly around your stomach or chin and now have a hanging fold that just bothers you, you might consult a plastic surgeon to see what can be done. Plastic surgery is usually not necessary, however, especially with weight loss of 20 to 30 pounds or less.

Does It Cost More to Diet?

Q. Reducing diets I've read about list foods that are high-priced and that I'm afraid I can't afford. Is this true of your diet program?

A. The answer to your question is a definite "no." The De-Betz Diet has very simple basic food items that will not cost you more than what you usually eat. If anything, I have found that once people start on a diet, their food bills go down because they cut out much of the expensive junk and fast food. They also buy less food for themselves.

A case in point involves an overweight family I treated some years ago. The family consisted of the parents and two teenage sons, all seriously overweight. After two months of my treatment, and consistent loss of weight by the entire family, the father reported triumphantly that since the family had been on my reducing diet program, their previously sky-high weekly food bill had been cut drastically. He added with a chuckle, "I even pay your office fee from the money that we save on food. It's incredible!"

Food-Handling Temptation

Q. As a cook in a restaurant, always handling food, I've failed to lose my huge overweight on other diets because I can't resist digging into the rich food. Will your diet program help me over that eating hurdle?

A. Being constantly around food obviously gives rise to more temptations, but if weight loss is important to you, you must make a commitment to separate your work from your desire to eat. Separation is the first step. Try to look at it this way: A person who works in a bank may want to have all that money that goes through his hands, but it would get him into serious trouble were he to take it. I'm sure you accept this point.

Now, look at the food in the restaurant in the same way: It's your work, separated from your personal desires. Digging into that rich, creamy nut dessert is actually a violation of work ethics. It's not there for you but for the patrons of the restaurant. Think about it.

Then use the touch-control action tool to help you keep your distance from the "forbidden" restaurant food. Touch . . . and that will stop you from sampling and overindulging. Make it a point not to eat while working. Take separate breaks for meals and eat a designated amount of food, not a morsel more. Once you establish the rules, such thin eating behavior will become your habitual way.

How to Help an Overweight Spouse

Q. I love my husband and am very fearful that his tremendous overweight might lead to a heart attack. He never lies except about food. For instance, I've seen him eat a giant box of cookies and yet he insists that he has eaten only one cookie. What can I do to get him to reduce?

A. I understand your concern about your husband's overweight and fear of a heart attack. Obviously, he has to be the one who decides ultimately to do something about his weight. Nagging usually doesn't help. However, you can help by not having cookies and candies so readily available. Cut up vegetables or fruit instead and offer it to him to nibble between meals. You may also want to talk to him about your anxiety, not in a nagging way but with sincere concern and care.

Then show him the way. Go through this book with him; have him read the touch-control instructions. Once he tries the "magic touch" and experiences the marvelous self-control effect, he'll be more amenable to going on the two-way program for a week. As he sees the pounds drop off, and feels so much better, he'll be on his way to a trimmer, healthier future.

Overcoming a Dieting "Plateau"

Q. After losing some weight on diets in the past for a week or two, I'd hit a plateau and stay the same—and then give up. Will your diet program overcome that?

A. Hitting a plateau is quite common during a weight-loss program, but doesn't happen to everyone, not by a long shot. So don't anticipate a plateau. Do keep in mind that your body is a very sensitive instrument, designed to function and maintain its most healthful weight—until abused. If you have restricted your food intake drastically for a couple of weeks, your body will think that there is not enough food available and will try to economize. Thus, it will probably slow down its metabolism, getting more mileage out of the same amount of food.

This is a very primitive and age-old mechanism in the chain of evolution, dating back to when man was still a hunter and cave dweller. Obviously, conditions are very different these days, but your body tends to respond in the same ancient way, not realizing that what you are doing is deliberate and with the best intentions for better health.

Here's what you can do about it: The most important factor is to avoid becoming frustrated and panicked. Use your touch-control tool to keep your motivation; fortunately, you now have this essential, effective aid that you never had before. Relax, but maintain your DeBetz Diet precisely as you skip the scale for a couple of days. In this special circumstance, it is important to give yourself a break and stop obsessing about numbers on the scale—but keep firmly in mind that as you just continue to feed your body right, according to my exact instructions, your weight will go down, even though at times it might reach a plateau.

If you want to overcome the plateau problem very quickly, undertake these two steps:

1. Set aside a day for fasting. Very simply, don't eat, but drink plenty of water, giving your body, which has cooperated faithfully to lose weight, a day of rest. It will respond favorably. Water has no calories, and the fasting day will definitely bring your weight down (see more instructions in the question-and-answer that follows).

2. Step up your activity level, increasing your metabolic rate and thus burning extra calories. Furthermore, check your salt intake and cut down on salty food if you're overdoing it; that can help.

My two-way touch-control program is especially designed to support you through any difficult impasses. Keep repeating the touch procedures, and you'll feel relaxed and refreshed each time. And, as noted before, the keys to success are patience, persistence and commitment. Again, touch . . . and soon your weight will go down steadily again.

To Fast or Not to Fast?

Q. Do you favor fasting at all?

A. I'm definitely not against a day of fasting for overweight individuals on my two-way weight-loss program. Such a day's vacation can be a relief to the system, and also may spur and speed the loss of excess pounds. Some people under my guidance like to fast one day a week. However, fasting is not necessary with the DeBetz Diet.

A day of fasting can be refreshing if you ever feel bloated and overfull due to overeating or for any other reason. It can also help break the cycle if you reach a plateau in losing weight. Those who fast for a day usually do it on Monday after eating excessively over the weekend. The choice is entirely yours whether to fast or not, and which day of the week you prefer. When you're overweight, your body feeds on your excess fat, so you shouldn't feel weak or tired. On the contrary—most people who fast claim that it gives them a "lift."

If you have any uncertainty at all about fasting, phone your doctor for an OK. Then, if approved, follow this simplest of fasting routines:

Don't eat anything; drink water only, and plenty of it. Your body needs the liquid to keep washing waste out of your system. Drink at least 12 or more 8-ounce glasses of water during your waking hours on your fasting day—a total of 12 or more, not necessarily at regularly spaced intervals.

If your reaction to this is "Oh no, I can't drink 12 glasses of water in a day," think again. Can you drink a glass of water an hour? Of course you can. Or can you drink half a glass of water each half-hour? That's a cinch, isn't it? Add it up—a glass of water an hour would be 16 glasses in 16 waking hours, still leaving you 8 hours of sleep without drinking.

If you prefer, you could drink that much liquid on your fasting day in a variety of no-calorie beverages—water, seltzer, sugar-free carbonated beverages, caffeine-free tea and coffee, and unsweetened herb teas. However, I recommend primarily the easiest and proved effective way—plain, unadulterated water, 12 glasses or more a day.

If you fast, I suggest that you limit your physical activity, not going beyond what is required routinely at work or home. You might also enjoy a comfortable walk, if you like. Do take a vitamin-mineral tablet for sure on your fasting day. But again, you don't have to fast on my weight-loss and maintenance programs. And don't increase your diet eating by loading up the next day; use touch-control to help keep you in line.

Overweight and Sex—Woman

Q. My husband says that if I take off my 20 pounds of overweight, we'll have a much better sex life. Is that true—does overweight really diminish sexual enjoyment?

A. Yes, it is true that, in general, people who have gained weight don't enjoy sex as much as before. The main reason is that the person feels bad about her body, so she becomes more self-conscious. This tends to interfere with free-floating, most satisfying sex for both partners.

It has been found too that if men gain a lot of weight, it may interfere with their libido (sex drive) and make them less interested and active sexually. This is probably due to a combination of psychological, physical, and mechanical factors. It can be very uncomfortable for a normal-weight woman to have sex in the missionary position (man on top) if her partner is overweight.

For example, if the partner gained the weight because she or he has been eating out of depression, then it's the depression that causes the primary lack of sexual desire and interest. For a variety of reasons, extreme weight gain usually (not always) results in the individual's getting less gratification from sex.

Overweight and Sex—Man

Q. I've gained a lot of weight in the past year, and I notice that some women I go for shy away from me at parties and bars. Could it be that my being a fat man now is interfering with my sex life?

A. Yes; reread the preceding question and answer. In addition, it's sad but true that most women shy away from very heavy men. Unfortunately, and perhaps unfairly, in our thin-oriented society the fat person, male or female, is discriminated against more often than not. You might be the finest gentleman inside, but if your appearance is not appealing, or is even repugnant, you cut yourself off from some encounters that could potentially lead to desirable intimacy and sex.

Overweight Teenagers

Q. I know that your diet program is for adults—but what can I do about reducing my overweight teenagers, a son of thirteen and daughter of fifteen?

A. Overweight teenagers may suffer from a number of physical and psychological problems. If not controlled now, the excess weight may persist into adult life. I strongly recommend that you take your children for a medical examination to rule out any of the physical ailments associated with overweight during adolescence. These include carbohydrate intolerance, increased or decreased secretion of insulin, thyroid, or other hormones, and more possibilities. In addition, overweight usually imposes a psychological burden on the growing individual due to disapproval and teasing from peers, and development of a poor self- and body-image.

Once you have checked with your family doctor about the above-mentioned conditions, I see no reason why your two teenagers should not go on my diet (ask your physician). It is a balanced diet and provides enough of all necessary nutrients. As I stress in these pages for adults, it is also of utmost importance to encourage your children to change their eating habits as taught here. This is especially vital in the early years, since one generally carries forward the habits developed at this phase of life.

You may also help your teenagers with your own example of healthy eating habits. Make sure that your refrigerator contains healthful foods instead of high-calorie and fast foods, which are usually high in fat and salt. Above all, have your youngsters checked regularly by the pediatrician or family physician, as you do for yourself.

Does a Sauna Take Off Weight?

Q. I go to a health club every week, and I lose 2 to 3 pounds in the sauna. Could I lose my 15 pounds overweight by going every day?

A. No! It would be outright dangerous to undergo the sauna and steam room every day. The temporary weight loss from sweating should not be confused with the true weight loss that results from a properly followed diet program.

Water Pills for Reducing?

Q. I hear that water pills are good for reducing. Is that so?

A. This should be understood about "water pills" (diuretics): For many women who are water retainers, doctors may prescribe diuretics, often to help control blood pressure, but not as a reducing agent. If women who retain excess water during the premenstrual period take water pills, they may lose the excess water temporarily. This should not be confused with true body weight. If you are generally overweight, and want to be trim permanently, my two-way reducing program will work for you and keep overweight from coming back.

Does Massage Reduce Weight?

Q. In the health club I go to, some women take a weekly massage after they exercise. The masseuse of that club claims that her customers lose up to a half-inch each time they get massaged. Can massages make you lose weight without dieting?

A. No. A massage makes you feel good and relaxes your muscles, especially if you're tense or after exercise. Enjoy a massage if you like. But the only one who might lose some weight during a massage is the masseuse, because she's the one who is burning off calories.

Should I Keep a Food Diary?

Q. What do you think of the value of keeping a daily food diary of what I eat? I hate to take the time and trouble—is it really worthwhile?

A. As you eat according to my diet, there's no need to keep a food diary because you have a clear daily listing to follow, and your calorie intake has been preplanned for you. After you have lost your overweight and don't follow my diet on a daily basis any more, but are using the blueprint directions, you might like to keep a diary, although it should not be at all necessary. Just follow the blueprint rules.

If you like to be more aware of the foods that you are eating, and can sit down periodically to calculate how many calories a day you eat, do it, of course. It may make you more aware of "hidden" calories, such as extra tastings from a friend's plate at dinner and bites of high-calorie foods while cooking a meal.

But since, as you say, you "hate to take the time and trouble," forget about a daily food diary, which sounds good theoretically but which very few people can maintain accurately and consistently. Use your touch-control action tool to keep from overeating, and watch that five-pound warning signal on the scale. You'll stay trim forever.

Does Exercising Assure Weight Loss?

Q. I don't understand why I've been gaining weight over the last couple of years. I've been exercising on a regular basis, and if I binge, I even add an extra mile of jogging. Can you explain to me what's happening?

A. Regular exercise is a healthy life-style habit, but it is not a way of weight control. It is true that exercise speeds up the metabolism and increases the burning up of calories, but it would take an enormous amount of exercising to counteract a binge of a few thousand calories (see chapter 10). An extra mile of jogging will not make up for a pint of vanilla fudge ice cream. Keeping your body nicely trim takes a combination of a sensible balanced diet and regular exercise.

"Must I Diet Always?"

Q. It's frightening to me to think that I may have to be on a diet always. Is that necessarily so?

A. We all diet, so to speak, except that some diets, that is, daily eating, add up to too much food, resulting in overweight. But with my two-way touch-control and diet program, you learn to eat in a healthful, balanced way that keeps your weight at a specific desired level. First you take off your excess weight, then you keep it off by adhering to my lifelong stay-trim blueprint. Look at your daily eating from the new perspective you have learned in the preceding pages. Then your stay-trim food intake loses any "don't eat and don't do" aspect. It becomes a healthful, satisfying way of life.

Must Aging Mean Gaining Weight?

Q. Does getting older automatically mean that I'll put on weight?

A. That's a fallacy, deceptive and misleading. When people get older, they may burn up less energy because they are physically less active and because the metabolism may slow down somewhat. But in general, overweight is simply the result of eating more food and calories than needed—at any age.

Are Diet Pills Desirable?

Q. I have a friend who says she lost a lot of weight because she took some kind of diet pills. Do diet pills really make you lose weight?

A. Certain diet medications act on a person's brain to suppress the appetite. If used in conjunction with a sensible diet, under a physician's supervision, they may be useful in the early phase of a weight-reduction program. But in themselves they don't make you lose weight. No matter what else, you ultimately have to restrict your food intake and make a firm, enduring commitment to the right weight-reduction and maintenance program.

Calories Don't Count?

Q. Some diets proclaim that "calories don't count." Is this true?

A. Wrong. Every calorie counts. If you are overweight, your excess pounds and dimensions result from consuming more calories than your body can use with the limited energy that you expend. In other words, when you take in more calories in eating than you expend in daily living, your system packs this excess fat into fat pockets, and your body swells and bulges. Indeed, every calorie counts, but you don't count calories on the DeBetz Diet because the daily calorie total is precounted for you.

Vitamin-Mineral Tablet Daily?

Q. Do I need a balanced diet even though I take a multi-vitamin-mineral tablet every day?

A. A balanced diet of carbohydrates, protein, and some fat is essential for good health. A balanced diet also gives you the necessary fiber, and supplies you with natural vitamins, minerals, and trace elements that are necessary for your body. Vitamins or minerals taken in excess or in the wrong combinations may even harm you. A daily vitamin-mineral tablet may be taken if you like, although it is not essential. But before you take large amounts of supplements, check with your doctor.

No Weight Loss on 600 Calories?

Q. An extremely overweight friend says she went on a 600-calorie diet and still didn't lose a pound. She's not tiny—she's over five feet tall. How could this be possible?

A. It is very unlikely that anyone who goes on a 600-calorie diet does not lose weight. Your obese friend is undoubtedly not fully aware of what she is eating. If she were to keep an accurate food diary, you'd probably find that she is taking in many hidden or "unaware of" calories, and that she is deceiving herself.

If she really consumes only 600 calories and doesn't lose weight, she may very likely have some physical malfunction. She should go to her doctor at once for a thorough medical checkup to rule out any thyroid underfunctioning or the like. If she is in normal health, I'll wager that she'll lose weight on the DeBetz Diet, eating between 900 and 1,200 calories.

Listen to Stomach Talk?

Q. I heard somebody who claimed to be a nutritionist say on the radio that you should listen to what your stomach asks for—and then feed it accordingly. I'm puzzled, since my stomach usually "asks for" a chocolate sundae or something rich like that. Is it correct that I should then eat the chocolate sundae or whatever my sweet tooth asks for? I actually heard this advice!

A. The only person who has a stomach that can talk is the ventriloquist; no other person's stomach can talk. The stomach can only give you signals of hunger, emptiness—or satiety, fullness. Everything else comes from your head and is a desire or an appetite to eat.

I point out to my patients, as I have informed you in detail earlier, that a good way of differentiating between real physical hunger and an appetite is this: When you're hungry, you just have a gnawing sensation in your stomach. An appetite is usually characterized by asking for specific rich food, such as having a strong desire for a chocolate sundae or a piece of salami or whatever else.

This is the important primary lesson for you: If you respond to an appetite, without being hungry at the time, you probably will overeat. In such situations, the touch-control concentration signal helps you to distinguish between hunger and desire, aids you in making the right choice, keeps you from breaking your diet or blueprint, and stops you from overloading.

Reducing Problem After Pregnancy

Q. I gained a lot of weight while having a baby, and now, months later, I'm having difficulty getting rid of the excess pounds. Will your diet program help me even though other diets haven't helped?

A. Yes, the two-way touch-control method will definitely help you lose the excess weight you have gained since you had your baby. Don't be concerned that you have tried other diets which haven't worked. If you follow my instructions carefully, you will lose. The success of my patients after having a baby proves it.

The reason it might have been difficult for you so far to lose weight is probably twofold: First, during pregnancy your appetite increased and you ate more. As you know, a 20-pound weight gain during pregnancy is a usual occurrence. If you gained much more than that, you probably overate during those months. Then, once the baby was delivered, the excess weight obviously stayed.

Second, if you breast-fed afterward, your appetite continued to be increased. Your body actually needed more food. Also, it could metabolize the food more efficiently because certain hormones were at work during that period.

Now that you are back to normal, your metabolism is back to normal as well, and your eating must go back to prepregnancy proportions. However, I strongly suspect that your eating habits have drastically changed, so that now you find it difficult to go back to the way you ate before, to a thin way of eating. That's why the diets alone did not work.

However, I'm convinced that the DeBetz Diet—in combination with the touch-control action tool—will help you shift back to a thin way of eating. You'll learn gratefully that touch-action is at your fingertips always to stop you from overeating and breaking your diet.

If you follow my program precisely and still don't lose your excess pounds, you should consult with your family doctor. Your physician will check for any physical malfunction. On my low-calorie diet, weight loss should follow as surely as day follows night.

Lose Weight, Lose Personality?

Q. People say they like me because I'm a "jolly fat man." My doctor tells me to take off 25 pounds, but I'm afraid I'll lose my personality. What do you think?

A. Probably the most pointed comment about that is by a popular overweight actress who decided to take off her unhealthy excess poundage. She said, "People tell me not to lose weight, that I might lose my personality. I tell them, 'Honey, it ain't in my thighs.'"

Similarly, your personality and character are in you, not in your swells and bulges. As a "jolly thin man," you should be more vigorous, attractive, and with a far better prospect of improved, enduring health.

14

ANSWERS TO RELATED DIET AND HEALTH QUESTIONS

To Aid Your Understanding for Enduring Weight Control

In the course of my medical practice, in addition to questions arising primarily from patients' personal concerns, I'm often asked about matters relating to allover health considerations. A good many queries seek my professional views on timely issues directly or indirectly involving overweight. I believe that the answers here will be of interest and value to you, too.

Smoking and Weight

Q. My family pressures me to stop smoking, but I am afraid to because I'm concerned about my weight. I've heard that people who stop smoking gain a lot of weight. What are the facts?

A. It's a fact that smoking is dangerous to health, and it's also a fact that overweight is harmful to health. To smoke and to be overweight, too, increases the health dangers. You definitely should determine to stop smoking, and also to keep your weight at a normal level.

You probably didn't know that nicotine alters the metabolism in only a small percentage of people. However, nicotine acts as a mild diuretic (water pill) to increase the amount of water your body excretes. Thus, when you stop smoking and cut down your nicotine intake, there is a short period, usually about 48 hours, of water retention. That results in an increase in the number of pounds when you step on the scale. Soon after, your weight returns to its previous level.

I have treated many patients who came to see me to help them stop smoking. I taught them a form of the touch-control method as an effective aid to keep from reaching for and lighting up a cigarette. I have found in my medical practice, in addition to national research results, that most people usually keep their weight as before, once they stop smoking. Others who gain weight do so predominantly for the following reasons:

1. They substitute one bad habit for another, namely, excessive eating. Instead of lighting a cigarette as in the past, they stuff candies, cookies, and other foods into their mouths each time they would have lit a cigarette in the past. As a result, they gain weight, of course. Also, many people would use a cigarette as a way of restricting their food intake. Instead of an appetizer or a dessert or a snack, the smoker would light up a cigarette. Naturally, if you replace no-calorie cigarettes with a high-calorie appetizer, dessert, or snack, the odds are that you are going to gain weight.

2. After a while, when you have stopped smoking, your taste buds improve and food tastes more delicious. This may lead to eating more than before—and again your weight increases.

3. I have also found that a number of the ex-smokers unconsciously gain the weight in order to have a "good" reason to return to smoking. This is especially true of women smokers. I've often heard statements such as "I'd rather smoke and worry about lung cancer than be heavy and unattractive. When I smoked, I was slim. Then I gained weight alarmingly, and that's why I went back to smoking."

With most individuals, the return to smoking doesn't get rid of the excess pounds—and again the person is stuck with two dangerous health problems: smoking and overweight. Here is your solution: You can stop smoking without becoming concerned about gaining weight. Just make sure that you follow my two-way program precisely—using the "magic touch" and the DeBetz Diet. Apply the touch-control action tool even more frequently than usual.

In this case, to keep yourself from lighting up a cigarette, say these smoking/eating STOPlines to yourself:

For my body, cigarette smoking and
overeating are both an insult and a poison.
I need my body to live.
I owe my body this respect and protection.

The peak-concentration benefit you get with the entire touch-control procedure will help you give up both cigarettes and overeating. I urge you to review both the STOPlines method in chapter 2 and the SUPPORTlines process in chapter 3.

Cancer and Diet

Q. There's a history of breast cancer in my family. My husband is very much concerned about cancer, too. We're told that the right way of eating might cut down the risk of getting cancer. Is your diet, or any other, an anticancer diet?

A. There are numerous studies of obesity and cancer that indicate a probable linkage. One of the largest studies, carried out by the American Cancer Society, involved more than one million men and women. The results are significant in answering you: Overweight males had a higher incidence of cancer of the colon, rectum, and prostate than men of average weight. Overweight females had a higher incidence of cancer of the gallbladder, biliary passages, breast, uterus, and ovaries than women of average weight.

The American Cancer Society has studied the food intake of these groups carefully and has found that the overweight women and men consumed, in general, a higher proportion of fat in their daily diets than those of average weight. As a result, the American Cancer Society now urges people to eat less fat and more fruits and vegetables. If you write to the Society, they will send you literature with more specific information.

Obviously, a low-fat diet like the DeBetz Diet, or any other, cannot cure cancer, but it can be regarded as preventive to some degree. There seems to be little question that a well-balanced low-fat diet provides greater safety in regard to cancer as well as many other ills.

Specifically regarding breast cancer, the American Health Foundation in New York has a special project for women who either had cancer or fall into a high-risk group for breast cancer. The undertaking includes a specific diet, very low in fat, along with a follow-up program.

In addition, scientific findings reveal that women with cystic breast disease have many fewer problems when they eliminate fats, chocolate, caffeine, and the like from their diets. All these facts are significant in affirming a vital relationship between diet and cancer. I must stress again that while no diet can promise definite cancer prevention or cure, any low-fat diet is, in effect, an anticancer diet. Frequent medical checkups are essential.

Fish Oil a Miracle Element?

Q. Every so often I hear about some new "miracle" food or element that you just swallow and then you become thin almost overnight. Lately I've read unbelievable claims about something called "Omega-3 Fish Oil." It sure doesn't sound appetizing. Is it really a wonder worker for losing weight?

A. If ever you see any product advertised as "instant" weight loss, or promising that you'll lose 10 pounds overnight without effort just by ingesting this or that potion, or by any other means—beware! There are no miracle drugs or other shortcuts. If you want to lose weight healthfully, go on a reduced-calorie program of balanced diet and exercise.

As long as people have had weight problems, there have been ourtrageous promises of miracle solutions to mislead us into believing we can lose weight without effort. Some of these sensational offerings can be very dangerous and even lethal. Not long ago, "liquid protein" was hailed as a miracle cure for overweight. After numbers of people were lured into buying and using the products, several deaths were reported in connection with their use.

Specifically regarding your question, Omega-3 is a lipid found in fish oil, which is extremely high in calories. Some experiments have stated that factors in fish oil, including Omega-3, have been found to lower cholesterol in humans. There are reports also of an effect on blood clotting. These accounts, a number of the scientists involved emphasize, are indicative, not conclusive.

One of the reasons Omega-3 has been related to weight loss is that societies that have high amounts of fish, thus fish oil, in their diets have a lower occurrence of obesity. But there is a catch: This has been found mainly in Japanese people and Eskimos whose diet consists predominantly of raw fish. Significantly, it also has been revealed that once these cultures adapt to the general American way of eating, *they are as prone to obesity as anybody else.* Thus, the assumption that raw fish and fish oils in any diet can control weight is questionable at best.

It is a fact that fish is healthful, low in calories, and an excellent source of protein. Fish is included plentifully in the DeBetz Diet. However, we cannot assume that ingesting large amounts of one ingredient found in cultures that are trim will solve our weight problems.

The claims of exceptional effect or safety of Omega-3 have not been substantiated by medical and bariatric professionals; possible dangers have been emphasized in authoritative reports. Before firm research data about the effects on humans of any new substance have been established, for weight loss or otherwise, caution is definitely indicated.

Do Brain Mechanisms Control Eating?

Q. I keep reading and hearing more and more that there are special "brain mechanisms" that control eating and weight. I'm confused by many terms I don't understand—such as "neurotransmitters," a hormone called "cholecystokinin," also elements named "tryptophan," "serotonin," and others. Should I learn what these mean to help control my weight?

A. Much scientific research by qualified professionals is going on steadily about weight control. Important findings will undoubtedly emerge. I'm not surprised that you're confused about the terms you mention, since a good many scientists are also. They're constantly testing, seeking answers, striving to break through to helpful new discoveries to improve health for humankind.

My recommendation is that you wait for clear, proved scientific findings. Don't be duped or misled by any opportunists who may seek to take advantage of your confusion for their own purposes. They may tell you that you must eat A before B and after C, interspersed with strict amounts of E and F, in order to arrive at miracles of weight loss and health improvement.

If you decide that you want to lose your excess weight, your best course, according to most authorities, including myself, is to go on a balanced, calorie-restricted diet that offers a variety of normal, readily obtainable foods. That's the basis of healthful weight loss. To that I add my touch-control method, tested and proved in my medical practice. The twofold purpose and result is to keep you from falling off your diet so that you reach your desired weight goal and then to help you stay trim lifelong.

How Much Salt Consumption?

Q. I've read a great deal about salt and its bad effects on health and weight. Should I cut out all salt in going on your diet?

A. Some salt (sodium chloride, NaCl) is essential for the human body. Nevertheless, as with so many other things, if you overdo your salt intake, it can be very dangerous to your health. I definitely recommend cutting down on salt when dieting—and lifelong.

Excessive salt consumption has been linked with increased high blood pressure, especially in those who already have a family predisposition relating to this problem. Too much salt intake also causes increased water retention in some people, thus bringing their weight up. This might seem rather inconsistent, since the human body should be well hydrated, that is, have a substantial amount of water in the tissues.

However, this is different from *retained* water, which is usually trapped in certain "loose" body spaces such as legs, face, hands, and fingers. An individual may be dehydrated at times, yet retain water in those spaces. The more salt a person consumes, the more water will be retained, leading to a swelling, bloated look.

Much has been written about the hidden dangers of salt in your food. It's true that we are not fully aware of all the foods that may include more salt than we realize. Among these sources are fast foods offered in popular eateries, and many canned, processed, and frozen foods that contain loads of salt of which we're not aware. Many packaged low-calorie foods and dinners are extremely high in sodium content—be wary.

It's important to read the labels on packaged foods before buying them. Look for the sodium content and compare with other packages in the same food category, including those labeled "low-sodium" or "sodium-reduced," which could be misleading unless you check. Reputable food processors will welcome your checking.

As a rule of thumb, remember this: You usually get enough salt to cover your daily requirements from foods as they are—fish, poultry, meats, vegetables, and so on—other than packaged products. There is no need to add sizable amounts of salt from the shaker, so break the salt-shaker habit when dieting and at any time.

Also, it's more healthful to cook without adding salt. Instead, flavor deliciously with herbs, spices, nonsalt seasonings, and lemon juice. I don't even remember the last time I purchased a package of salt. I never add salt to my food, but I'm not fanatic about it, nor do I suggest that you be unless you're restricted by your doctor's orders.

You'll notice that once you eliminate added salt from your diet, you'll soon become very sensitive to salty foods, and you'll find them undesirable, even distasteful. It's my experience, and my dieting patients and health-minded friends agree, that the less salt added, the more you're able to appreciate the fine inherent flavors of good foods—another gourmet benefit.

Salt and Dieting

Q. In the past when I've gone on a reducing diet, I lose pounds the first few days, and then the weight stops dropping. Has salt intake anything to do with this?

A. Most reducing diets eliminate added salt, so for the first few days your salt consumption will drop. As a result, you usually eliminate a sizable amount of retained water, and your weight goes down. This is generally temporary, as your body stabilizes.

The same effect is seen when you take a "water pill" (diuretic). Obviously, if you stop taking the diuretic, or go back on high-salt foods, you will retain more water, and your weight will go up. However, this water is not true weight. Some women retain as much as five pounds of water premenstrually; again, this is not real weight gain, but increased water in the body, which adds to the weight that you read on the scale. Frequently women use this menstrual condition as an excuse if they haven't lost enough weight. Sometimes a patient claims while stepping on my office scale, "I'm expecting my period, that's why I haven't lost any weight." I accept this statement once, but not all the time!

I remind people with a questionable excuse to follow touch-control and DeBetz Diet instructions precisely, and they will lose weight over both the short and long run—regardless of menstruation and other problems. The next time they call or visit me, they always report that the weight has dropped very satisfactorily. If the problem persists, I advise a medical checkup by the personal physician or a specialist.

"Natural" Foods and "Health" Foods

Q. Are so-called natural foods and health foods really natural and healthful, better than other foods not designated that way?

A. Unfortunately, it ain't necessarily so. As with salt content, you must read labels carefully before buying packaged foods. Check for calories and nutrients, listed on packages increasingly. Don't believe overall designations such as "light," "low-calorie," and "natural" without reading the list of ingredients carefully. "Natural" can be particularly misleading, as is "health food." Once a product is processed and packaged, is it truly "natural"? Furthermore, a number of nature's poisons are "natural," yet potentially deadly. Also, is a "health" food healthful for everyone just because it is so named?

There are many reputable food manufacturers, processors, and packagers—but there are also many who seek to get away with anything they can. The motto of the latter is "Let the buyer beware." So do beware; don't accept that a food is "light" or "lower in calories" without checking the ingredients list.

Is Calcium Needed?

Q. Everywhere I turn I read and hear health advisers saying, "Eat more calcium, more, more." Is calcium a magical health potion? Can you clear up the confusion for me?

A. Calcium is a necessary mineral in the diet. The Recommended Daily Allowance is 800 milligrams for men and women, and higher for middle-aged women, approximately 1,000 milligrams (1 gram). But here, as with any other nutrient, moderation is indicated. New evidence indicates that too much of this mineral might do more harm than good.

Calcium is necessary to develop strong bones, but calcium alone will not prevent the development of diseases like osteoporosis. There are many other factors involved. Here are just a few points to keep in mind:

No matter how much calcium you consume or take in supplements, your body might not be absorbing it properly if you drink excessive amounts of alcohol or coffee, or are taking certain diuretics on a regular basis.

If you had stomach surgery, and food passes through your body too quickly to be properly absorbed, the calcium in your food will also not be absorbed properly. If your system cannot tolerate dairy products, a major source of dietary calcium, you may have to substitute other foods high in calcium.

In addition, there are indications that heavy smokers and women who don't exercise are more prone to develop osteoporosis. Preventive measures against possible calcium deficiency include eating plenty of foods that supply natural amounts of calcium. If necessary, consider taking supplements. Make sure that you get plenty of regular exercise, and avoid those factors that cause malabsorption of the mineral. Before you take calcium supplements, check with your doctor.

How Much Fiber?

Q. Everybody seems to be pushing the idea that the only way to be really healthy is to eat a lot of fiber. I have a very sensitive stomach and I'm concerned. Is it necessary to consume a lot of fiber every day?

A. At a symposium on Food and Nutrition in Health and Disease of the New York Academy of Sciences, it was concluded that the effects of dietary fiber in man are still not fully known. Some beneficial effects are observed when fiber is added to the diets of animals that are fed special diets. Some claims have been made regarding the role of fiber in relation to cancer of the colon, stating that diets high in fiber may have a protective effect on the colon.

However, too much fiber, especially if coming from "fiber pills" or excessive amounts of bran, may cause obstruction and blockage in the gut. As in any other area of nutrition, *moderation* is the key word. Here are a few guidelines for an adequate intake of dietary fiber:

Eat different types of foods that are known to be high in fiber, including whole grains, fresh fruit, fresh vegetables, beans, seeds, and nuts. Chew on tasty raw vegetables and fruits rather than cooked. Don't overcook your vegetables. Edible skins are a good source of fiber, too. Fiber acts as a natural laxative, so if you suffer from chronic constipation, perhaps you don't eat enough fiber. Also, you may not drink enough water. These two elements, water and fiber, are prime contributors to proper elimination of waste material.

Effect of Antidepressant Medication

Q. Help! Since I've been taking an antidepressant medication, my weight has gone up, even though I haven't increased my food intake. That makes me even more depressed. What should I do?

A. A rise in weight occurs occasionally when individuals take certain antidepressant medications. They may have an influence on your metabolism. Some people lose weight and others gain. If you've gained some weight and are unhappy about it, go on the DeBetz Diet plus the touch-control procedures—that's basic and essential. Also, increase your activity level. You should soon be delighted with your slimmed body.

If, for whatever reason, you cannot get your weight under control, discuss it with your doctor, and with him or her weigh the benefits of the antidepressant medication along with its side effects. Sometimes all it takes is to switch to a different kind of medication.

Faulty Metabolism?

Q. I think I must have a faulty metabolism that makes me so overweight. Can your diet program overcome that problem?

A. As I pointed out at the beginning of this book, before you go on this or any other diet, you should check with your doctor. Your physician is the only one who can determine if there is anything wrong with your metabolism. There are tests available that can answer these questions, so that you don't have to wonder and worry.

Once you have your physician's approval, you can go on my diet at once, and with the added booster effect of the touch-control action tool, you should have no problem about losing your excess weight and keeping trim from now on. Please keep in mind, however, that no diet will cure a physical problem, so a medical examination is essential.

Menopause's Effect on Weight

Q. Is it true, as friends tell me, that it's especially difficult to keep weight down after menopause, which I'll be approaching soon?

A. No, it is not difficult if you keep to your touch-control and diet method of eating. The hormonal changes that take place during menopause may change your metabolism to a certain degree, but if you keep physically active and in good spirits, there should be no fear of gaining.

Most women who gain weight during this period of time frequently overeat because of depression. As you may know, a certain percentage of women who go through menopause have a difficult time adjusting to this period of life, and may suffer from some depression. They are concerned about the end of fertility, and may feel mistakenly that they might not be as attractive as before, or as adequate sexually.

In a percentage of women, this is a difficult period of life, and food sometimes represents to them solace and soothing. All this is a misconception and should be cleared up. I strongly suggest that if you feel uneasy at all, talk to your family doctor or gynecologist; perhaps having psychotherapy will help you go through this phase. I must emphasize that menopause, understood thoroughly, can be an uplifting new beginning rather than an ending.

In regard to your specific query about losing weight, go on my two-way reducing program. Once you're down to your desired weight, follow the stay-trim blueprint precisely. It's more difficult to lose if you let yourself go over your five-pound limit. That's true whether after or before menopause, and at any age.

Anorexia

Q. During the past year I've dropped over 20 pounds. Although my friends tell me that I'm anorexic, I still feel fat and would like to lose even more. Dieting is very easy for me and at times I go days without eating. Do you think I am an anorectic? If so, what can I do about it?

A. Anorexia nervosa is a serious illness that can lead to death; 10 percent of anorectics die as a result of this eating disorder. The affliction is characterized by an excessive desire to lose weight. Sometimes it starts out with the child, teenager, or young adult having some overweight and wanting to lose it. Once dieting, the individual cannot stop dieting out of fear of gaining again. This is usually accompanied by a distortion of body image. Even though the individual is extremely thin, she still thinks of herself as being fat.

I have treated anorexic patients by teaching them the touch-control method to help them eat properly. Clearly, it is as much of an insult to the body to withhold adequate food as it is to overstuff it. If you should find, improbably, that your desire to lose more weight persists after you have reached your originally established weight-loss goal, you should consult your doctor at once, or go for psychiatric help. Anorexia is a complex illness, far beyond the general area of weight loss or gain.

Bulimia

Q. A friend in my college dormitory has a beautiful figure, yet she's the biggest eater I ever saw. She says she has bulimia and makes herself throw up right after eating. Is this bulimia a healthy, safe way to stay thin?

A. Bulimia is a serious disorder characterized by recurrent episodes of binge eating, often associated with self-induced vomiting or laxative abuse. The bulimic individual is usually of normal weight and almost proud of the fact that she can eat huge amounts without gaining weight. However, bulimia is very unhealthy and definitely not a way to control weight.

Bulimia has become almost a fashionable disease, from a distorted viewpoint. It is seen quite frequently among college students, although a small percentage in numbers. It is very dangerous, and is like being addicted to a potent, destructive drug. Once a person starts the vicious cycle of bingeing and vomiting, it is extremely difficult to get away from it.

The illness is also very dangerous for medical reasons. Due to the frequent vomiting, the body is depleted of very important electrolytes and minerals needed to regulate a variety of bodily functions, including heart function. Bulimia may even kill. You may remember the death of a very popular singer who reportedly died as a result of bulimia. One of the best-known movie stars struggled for many years to overcome her bulimic habits.

I have seen many bright young women who ruined their careers and social lives because of bulimia. Once hooked, the bulimic may start to get so obsessed and involved with food that there is no time to do academic or any other demanding work. She may start to neglect her friends, spending increasing amounts of time in her rituals of overeating and vomiting.

My advice is: *Stay away from bulimic actions.* Follow a proved reducing diet and program to lose excess weight. Above all, don't view bulimia as a desirable way to stay thin. The outcome can be tragic. If you're tempted, seek autoritative professional help at once.

Can a Balloon Cut Food Intake?

Q. I heard that there is a new method of putting a balloon into the stomach, with the result that it makes you eat less. You feel full all the time. What do you think about this procedure?

A. The stomach balloon, as well as some other surgical procedures, is indicated only for people who are extremely overweight, have really tried "everything," and just cannot keep on a program. These drastic surgical measures are usually reserved for the pathologically obese person who has to lose for medical reasons but has failed repeatedly. Procedures like this should always be very thoroughly discussed with your doctor and a reputable specialist in that area.

Even if a procedure like this is judged to be indicated for you, the outcome is not always what was expected. I've seen patients who had their intestines bypassed, or their jaws wired, or subjected themselves to some other extreme procedure. Nevertheless, they managed to overeat and gain the weight back. The old saying holds true, "You cannot have your cake and eat it too." Before you undertake any such courses, have a second and a third and a fourth opinion by qualified specialists.

Lipectomy for Weight Loss?

Q. Can you explain what this new procedure called "lipectomy" is, and if it could help me lose my extreme overweight permanently?

A. Lipectomy is the suctioning of fat deposits from under the skin, using a tubelike vacuuming device. It is not a way of balanced weight reduction and is usually performed on those individuals who have unsightly pockets of fat that remain despite dieting and exercising. The procedure has not been used long enough for anyone to make definite statements on its safety and lasting effectiveness.

There have been reports of patients whose removed fat deposits came back. There have been numerous serious problems. Whatever way you look at it, weight reduction requires effort and commitment. There are no shortcuts. The DeBetz Diet and touch-control can help you to get down to your ideal body weight and keep it there. I urge you to try this program and stick with it before even thinking of undergoing an unproved surgical procedure such as lipectomy.

Physical Malfunction

Q. On every diet I've ever tried, and I've tried plenty up to now, I eat very little. Yet I don't lose weight, and often I even gain. Don't you agree that I must have a physical malfunction?

A. If you have any doubts about whether your body is functioning properly, check with your doctor. In general, if you go on a low-calorie balanced medical diet and add some regular activity as I recommend, your weight must definitely come down.

Many of my patients have had doubts like yours until they used my touch-control method and became aware of some personal hidden bad eating habits. One told me about a common hidden problem that emerged—unconscious night eating. She'd awaken, go to the bathroom, stop at the refrigerator on the way back, and gorge—but not remember it in the morning. Others load up on rich hors d'oeuvres at a party without realizing that they're consuming hundreds of extra calories.

My advice is that you go on my two-way diet confidently. Use the touch-control concentration procedures as directed, essential help you never had before. I'll bet that your excess pounds will come off and stay off. I'm certain because this dual program has worked for so many formerly overweight women and men I've helped.

Fear of Heart Attack

Q. A close friend, very overweight, joined one of those weekly diet groups, and after a few sessions he suddenly had a heart attack. I should diet to get rid of my fat and flab, but I'm afraid now. Have you any good advice for me?

A. There was probably no relationship between your friend's having a heart attack and going to weekly sessions at a diet group. His heart attack was probably long in the coming and he should have done something about his weight long ago.

In regard to your fear about losing weight and a heart attack, first consult your doctor before you start this or any other diet, as I've stated repeatedly. It's good medicine and reassurance to have an electrocardiogram and some basic blood tests before starting a weight-reduction program. That's especially needed if your goal is to lose more than just five or ten pounds.

Birth Control Pills and Weight

Q. Since I started taking birth control pills, I've been eating like mad and I've gained a lot of weight. Is there something in the pills that increases appetite—and could I control that on your diet program?

A. It's not unusual that women who go on the pill start gaining weight. For one thing, they may retain more water, so the numbers on the scale go up. If your weight increases, take a critical look at your food intake, and cut down somewhere. My recommendation is that for at least one week each month you go on the DeBetz Diet. Use the touch-contol procedures for extra, effective support.

Birth control pills have an influence on metabolic rate and water-retention mechanisms. If you find the weight gain, if any, a real problem, then you should assess the advantages against the negatives—and make your choice. Sometimes these weight changes are temporary, and once your body becomes adjusted to the pill, you'll be able to go back to your before-pill way of eating. As a dependable eating guide, then, follow my lifelong stay-trim blueprint, as many of my formerly overweight patients do, with enduring success.

Cholesterol Facts

Q. I'm about to start your DeBetz Diet, since a friend gave me a copy of your office leaflet, but I'm worried since I have a high cholesterol level in tests my doctor took. Is yours a high-cholesterol diet or not—and can you clarify basic cholesterol facts for me?

A. If your cholesterol level is high, you'll be happy to learn that my diet is relatively low in cholesterol, especially if you go on the meat-free variation of the basic diet. Without going into great detail, here are a few fundamental facts about cholesterol:

Cholesterol is a fatty substance that clogs the blood vessels and may lead to heart disease, as well as other vascular problems. There are different forms of cholesterol, including LDL and VLDL cholesterol. "LDL" stands for low-density lipoprotein. "VLDL" refers to very-low-density lipoprotetin. Both substances contribute to fatty deposits in blood vessels. Also, there is HDL, high-density lipoprotein, which helps to eliminate cholesterol from the body, thus having a "heart protective" function.

Medical evidence suggests that some people are more predisposed to developing high cholesterol levels than others. But it is also a known fact that certain foods, such as fatty meats, certain dairy products, and eggs, are high in cholesterol. They should be avoided by people who have a high level of cholesterol. Exercise also plays a role in helping lower it.

Olive Oil and Cholesterol

Q. I read that olive oil can lower levels of harmful cholesterol. Is that true?

A. Olive oil is a monounsaturated fat. Monounsaturated fats have been found to lower blood cholesterol and may be safer to eat than large amounts of polyunsaturated fats. The most common sources of monounsaturated fats are virgin olive oil and peanut oil. But these oils are not included in my diet, since they are very high in calories, and are neither desirable nor essential while on my reducing diet.

Six Feedings Daily?

Q. I read that if you divide the food you eat in three meals daily into six feedings instead, you'll lose weight faster. Is this true? Do you advise the six feedings instead of three meals?

A. It's not the number of meals that is most significant, but the total amount of calories you consume daily. However, physiologically, your body is set up in such a way that it functions most efficiently if there is a regular food intake, never an overload at one time.

For some people it is sufficient to eat two meals per day, for others three. A number of tests indicate that for some individuals, the metabolism works best if they eat the same total amount of food in six smaller meals rather than three. If your body is accustomed to eating three meals a day, I would suggest that you keep it that way. You will not lose more quickly or significantly by eating six meals instead.

It is more likely that a person switching from three to six feedings will increase the daily food total by eating more frequently. To repeat, the most desirable number of feedings differs from person to person. I recommend sticking to what has customarily worked best for you.

Water Loss

Q. Skeptics keep telling me, "There's no point in dieting since the only weight you lose is water, and it'll keep coming back." Is that true?

A. It's generally true that at the beginning of a diet, the dieter tends to lose a good deal of water. The reason is that usually your diet eliminates foods that contained a lot of salt, so there was a considerable amount of water retention in your body. Also, if you are on a diet and you drink a large amount of water, this too helps the body to eliminate much of the waste material, including retained water.

Note this all-important point: Not everyone loses a lot of water in starting a diet. If you do, then soon your body will be losing true weight. If you diet, lose pounds, and then maintain your weight goal, there's no need to worry that the water will come back. However, you will start retaining water, if that was your problem, if you go back to eating foods that are high in salt, or if you permit yourself to start gaining weight again. It's an established fact that, in most instances, the heavier a person is, the more prone to water retention that person is.

The bottom line is this: Don't be concerned about losing "only water," and don't use that as an excuse. Go on the DeBetz two-way reducing program. You'll take off pounds and inches steadily, and that will convince you that you're losing plenty of fat, not just water.

Sleep and Weight

Q. I need a lot of sleep, ten hours a night and an hour-long nap in the afternoon. Does all that sleep contribute to my being overweight?

A. Ten hours a night and an hour-long nap in the afternoon seems to be an excessive amount of sleep for most individuals. I suggest that you consult your family doctor to check for any special problems. There are some conditions in which hypersomnia (excessive sleeping) is part of the clinical picture —in depression, for instance.

Some people sleep more and thus avoid eating, and of course the sleeping in that case would not contribute to gaining weight. But if you sleep so much and eat your normal amount of food, or even more, then you will probably gain. The reason is that during sleep the metabolic rate is decreased, so you need less food than usual to maintain your body's weight. Excessive sleeping is not recommended in any case.

Skin Problems and Weight

Q. I've always had skin problems, but my skin is much
clearer since I slimmed down with your diet program. Is
there a connection?

A. Yes, there is a connection between clear skin and diet, as
affirmed by the clear complexions of many of my slimmed
patients. This correlation is often even more apparent in teenagers. Many people break out and develop skin blemishes if
they eat a lot of chocolate or foods high in fat or sugar. Since my
diet is low in fat and high in complex carbohydrates (natural,
not from sugars), that stimulates the drinking of a lot of water,
which helps the skin clear up. You'll welcome your skin improvement as a most desirable extra side effect of my diet.

Fad Diets

Q. I keep hearing about "fad diets" time after time, but I
don't understand—just exactly what is a "fad diet"?

A. Coauthor Samm Sinclair Baker answers: According to dic-
tionaries, *fad* basically means "temporary." So a fad diet is
literally one that lasts a very limited time, perhaps bizarre, often
one-dimensional, such as eating nothing but fruit or yogurt or
some other "magical" food. While the diet may catch on fast, it
usually fades away just as quickly.

Unfortunately, some enduring, effective diets have been
called "fad" by competitive so-called experts who criticize any
diet book as "fad" if it isn't their own—especially if they haven't
read the book. My experienced advice is that you read the details of any diet and decide for yourself. Also ask your doctor.

I Can't Give Up Wines and Liquor

Q. I've failed on diets up to now because while I can cut
down on eating, I can't give up the wines and liquor I
enjoy so much. Have you a solution for me?

A. If you have found it very difficult to cut out the alcohol, my diet is just right for you. You'll appreciate the fact that you are permitted to have three ounces of dry Champagne, sparkling wine, or dry wine every single day. Although this may be less alcohol than you usually drink, by allowing yourself this amount you will not feel deprived or frustrated. My patients have found this to be so, and they keep dieting until down to their desired weight.

But if you drink more than those three ounces of wine daily, you'll be breaking your diet. You won't lose your excess pounds as steadily, or at all perhaps, since once you start ignoring my diet instructions, you may go way above the daily calorie limit. Enjoy your three ounces of dry sparkling Champagne or other wine each day, sipping slowly, savoring each little swallow, as you keep dieting faithfully. You'll be delighted that you did when you're slim, attractive, and free of the unhealthy burden of overweight.

If you are an alcoholic, that's a different, very serious problem. You should seek specialized medical and other help immediately.

What Is "Cellulite"?

Q. I keep seeing ads on TV, and hearing advice from some so-called fitness experts exhorting people about special ways to get rid of cellulite on the body. What is cellulite, and what should I do about it? Do I need a special diet?

A. First, "cellulite" is a contrived commercial name for certain fat deposits on the body; it is not a medical term. With that in mind, the only way to get rid of "cellulite" is to lose weight. There are no magic potions, lotions, massages, or procedures that remove various common, unsightly fat deposits.

The body's fat is stored right beneath the skin, and connective fiber strands separate fat cells into different compartments. When the fat cells increase in size, they bulge out of these compartments, giving the skin the typical pebbled "orange peel" appearance. Whether or not you develop this condition depends mainly on the number of fat cells in your body, the strength of the connective fibers, and the thickness of your skin.

As we all know, there are special areas where people have the majority of their fat cells. In women that is primarily around their thighs, abdomen, and buttocks, and there's no miracle solution to remove resultant bulges. As stated plainly by the Medical Society of the County of New York in a recent paper: "Fat is fat. There is no medical condition known as 'cellulite.' And 'cellulite' can only be removed as any other fat by proper diet and exercise."

Pressures of Society

Q. I want to lose weight, but every time I start a diet I find myself bombarded by food ads on TV, radio, in newspapers and magazines, along with color photos and articles pushing rich, tempting food at me. So I succumb and start overeating again. I feel that the pressures of society are against me. Is there anything I can do to resist all that and fight back?

A. It's true that we live in a very food-oriented culture. It's equally true that we live also in a weight-conscious society. The message is mixed: On one hand, we are bombarded by food advertisements; on the other hand, we are flooded with images that tell us to be thin. You have a dilemma, but do you really think "society" is to blame for your overweight?

Here is the solution: Be a gourmet, which means that you enjoy food thoroughly, but in small amounts—and thus you keep losing weight and you trim down to the slim figure you want. The touch-control two-way method is exactly what you need to keep on your diet, taking off excess pounds in spite of outside pressures.

Once slim, you'll stay that way by following my lifelong stay-trim blueprint. You'll take pride in your accomplishment, and you'll laugh at the "pressures of society." After all, you're not "society"—you're an independent, self-respecting individual.

TO YOUR SLIM, HEALTHIER FUTURE

By following my instructions and recommendations throughout this book, you will slim down to your desired weight, and you'll never be overweight again. There's no question that you'll lose your excess weight and keep it off—unless you don't follow the directions accurately. Neither I nor Samm Baker can diet for you or apply the touch-control procedure for you. It's now up to you.

I have faith that you'll follow instructions and succeed splendidly—or you wouldn't be reading this book. Everything you need to succeed is in these pages. If you don't lose weight, you're doing something wrong. Go back and recheck chapters as needed. For details on any specific point, refer to the index. Like your touch-control action tool, this book is always at your fingertips with invaluable help.

From my medical experience, I know that excess weight, especially considerable extra poundage, often leads to physical and emotional problems and illnesses. But, while being slim is a great boon, it is in itself no guarantee of excellent health; sickness that has nothing to do with weight may occur.

Therefore I must stress again that you should have a medical checkup before going on this or any other diet. Also, contact your doctor if any negative symptoms occur. I urge you to have a physician's examination at least once a year to help prevent illness before it happens.

Above all, we wish enduring good health and increasing happiness and well-being for you and yours. . . .

ACKNOWLEDGMENTS

Grateful acknowledgment to:

Natalie Baker, invaluable, unflagging colleague in our heart-warming collaboration.

Oscar Dystel, brilliant partner, enduring friend.

Perry Knowlton, intelligent, esteemed associate.

James O. Wade, superlative editor, total professional.

And to all the others at Crown who contributed splendidly to this book.

INDEX